It Takes Two to Tandem

Louise George

It Takes Two to Tandem

Self-published with CreateSpace by Louise George

First edition published in November, 2013
ISBN: 10:1490928596
ISBN-13:978-1490928593

Cover design by Levi T George

Memoir, travel, cycling

For Nev
Thank you,
for never giving up on anything

Contents

Preface 7

Thurso – John O'Groats 8

John O'Groats – Armadale 17

Reminiscing 27

Armadale – Carbisdale Castle 36

Carbisdale Castle - Loch Ness.....................48

Loch Ness - Glencoe....................................53

Glencoe - Loch Lomond 65

Loch Lomond - Wanlockhead 72

Wanlockhead - Carlisle 84

Carlisle - Kirkby Lonsdale 91

Kirkby Lonsdale – Chester...........................108

Chester...113

Chester – Clun..116

Clun - Welsh Bicknor....................................121

Welsh Bicknor – Cheddar.............................126

Cheddar – Okehampton.................................135

Okehampton - St Austell...............................139

St Austell - Lands End - Penzance 144

Penzance – Worthing....................................152

London – Paris 156

Paris – Avignon 164

Avignon – Gordes..171

Gordes – Gordes 181

Gordes – Apt 186

Apt 190

Apt – Pernes-Les-Fontaines 192

Pernes-Les-Fontaines - Avignon..................197

Avignon – Milan 204

Milan - Florence 209

Florence - Radda in Chianti 217

Radda in Chianti - San Gimignano................226

San Gimignano - Siena 232

Siena 236

Rome...241

About the author 248

Acknowledgements 249

Part One

JOGLE
(John O'Groats to Lands End)

The Journey through Great Britain

approx. 70 miles

Preface

The riding is easy. I appreciate the comfortable start to this expedition. The narrow road is relatively flat, traffic is virtually non-existent and the only weight borne is our own.

I glance down at the tandem's name printed audaciously in silver text, along the thick, black, bottom tube, directly below me; '**Fandango**'. The tune from Queen's "Bohemian Rhapsody" jingles in my head. *'Scaramouch, Scaramouch, will you do the fandango?'* At this moment our Fandango is light and lively. I wonder, *'Over this journey will our Fandango resemble the romantic 'dance of friendship', or will the branding be synonymous with alternative definitions; 'a quarrel', 'a big fuss', or the more hopeful, 'brilliant exploit?'*

We are together, albeit one behind the other. Having now begun this great adventure; we are committed!

Thurso – John O'Groats

Day One
Wednesday, 6th June 2007
Getting Started

"**W**ow! You're here already. You must have ridden like a mad man?"

I had an inkling Nev would be waiting. He is always keen for a race. The challenge to beat me, travelling the same route by public bus, would be impossible for him to resist.

I had left the hostel in Thurso before Nev. The excuse of a bus to catch had let me off assisting with the last of the tandem reassembly. Anyway, Nev knows I am virtually useless when it comes to knowledge of bicycle technicalities. I have never had the desire, or the need, to be involved in the maintenance of the mountain bikes we usually ride. In fact I have rarely even used a tyre pump. There has been this unspoken agreement; whenever we returned home from a ride, usually near dinner time, Nev would wash the mud from both bikes and attend to any minor maintenance, while I attended to the children and meal preparations. He has always graciously responded to any comment from me, such as that my tyres seem to need some air, with a trip to the shed, pump in hand. So I left Nev tinkering with his links and screws and Allen Keys.

I changed into my Lycra cycle pants and top. A fluorescent yellow jacket, which a friend has kindly lent to me, adds warmth and a 'visibility layer'; not that I need to draw attention to myself on this part of the journey! For extra warmth and modesty on the bus ride, I have covered the Lycra knicks with new, beige, lightweight trousers; the first item of clothing I have ever purchased that is beige in colour! If I bump into Scottish comedian Billy Connolly while I am travelling though his homeland, I am sure he will be able to throw out a string of tandem jokes, and no doubt he will also jest about one of the riders being a member of the 'beige brigade'! (He coined the term, to identify the age-stage of women over 50, who are unable to make up their minds about the colour of a clothing purchase). My beige trousers though, are well cut, trendy après-ski wear. Always on the lookout for a bargain, I grabbed them from the 'end of season sale rack'. When I stepped outside the poky in-store changing room, and asked Nev for his opinion, he responded quite sincerely, but with just a trace in his tone of um, not so sure, "They make you look as if you have no backside."

"Wonderful!" My delight that they must be perfect changes Nev's expression to one of 'I must have missed something' as the purchase is made.

Fashion magazines espouse that the right attire can create a high degree of confidence. I'm not experiencing that spin off. Standing here with my Lycra disguised, I might be dressed for the part, but internally I am a tangled knot of nerves. I've been at the bus stop for what seems like ages. A constant stream of negative thoughts flows through my head. At this point I am not sure what is going to be the biggest challenge for me. Will my limb muscles be sufficiently honed to achieve the distance? I will be spending six weeks in the sole company of my husband, which in itself is likely to present some challenges. Nev will be my Captain; will he suffer silently through any of my weaknesses? My biggest fear though, is in relation to a condition that I had hidden from everyone for a number of years; not even daring to admit to myself that I had a problem. I'd braced myself recently, faced the fact that I had a problem and made Nev aware of my 'irritable bladder'. I hadn't intended confessing to this physical annoyance so early in my story, but how I was going to cope with urgent and frequent urinating, had been troubling me during the preparation for this trip.

Advertisements for 'Tena' products portray smiling attractive women of middle age. In spite of the branding, it implies that it is normal for women to experience 'leakage', when they go about activities such as jogging and bike riding. It is suggested that 'anything' can be quite cheerfully achieved with a 'pad' to disguise true degeneration. I was determined that I would not become a 'Tena' lady. In fact I disliked those advertisements so much, I decided only a matter of weeks ago that now was the time to seek expert advice. In spite of various medical consultations, no physical abnormality was diagnosed, and I was left with the conclusion that the irritating urgency was something brought about through poor mind training. Evidently my bladder has developed a response to my giving in to its impatient demands, like a spoilt tantrum-throwing two year old! The more my bladder demanded, the sooner I gave in, and the pattern was set. So at this point I have not resolved the 'bladder rules brain' conundrum. I'm really not sure how I will cope on a sixteen day journey, sitting on a bicycle seat!

The wait at the bus stop is much longer than I expect. Instead of thinking of the sensible explanation - that I have arrived too early - I begin feeling apprehensive, concerned that I may in fact have missed my ride.

Two particular situations cause my bladder strife; when I am nervous and when the air is cool. Both triggers are affecting me right now. The sensation is prickly and burning, and the irritation warns that an urgent 'discharge' will be the only solution that will bring relief. The railway station, from where the bus is to leave, houses the nearest public toilet. I 'yank the door' in earnest, but the sign facing me through the glass informs that the station is locked until early evening when the daily train is expected. I have no option but to apply well-proven coping mechanisms. Firstly, to 'jiggle and jiggle' with my entire body squeezed intensely, especially the toes curled tightly – believe me, it works! Visualise the antics of a busting child, minus the hand clutching the nether regions, and you'll get the picture. This is the best immediate solution. Reprimanding self-talk follows; *'You know you don't need to go, you went at the hostel. Focus on something else'.*

I am extremely relieved to be able to apply a 'distraction intervention'; the best 'toddler tantrum taming technique'.

I am joined by a couple of guys who arrive to wait for the bus. I have too much self respect to let my problem be publicly witnessed. Conversation is just what I need for my distress to fade into insignificance. They had yesterday completed the same journey that I am about to begin, albeit they rode from south to north. Yesterday they were too keen to finish their

11

adventure and hadn't taken the time to linger at John O'Groats. They are therefore now returning in the comfort of public transport, to do some sight-seeing in the vicinity.

The day is cool for early summer and I have chosen to sit on the sun filled side of the bus. The heater is on too, and the warmth mingles with the heat of the sun radiating through the glass. A cloying stuffiness causes my head to drop to my chest, as the combination of warmth, gentle motion, and a little jet-lag, lulls me into a travel stupor.

The bus route meanders away from the main road. The travel is slow and each time I sense a reduction in pace with the subsequent lowering of gears, I force at least one eye partially open, and convince my brain to engage significantly enough, to try to identify if by any chance we are overtaking a 'sole tandem rider'. My narrow view is only of clusters of ancient stone cottages bordering the stretch of tarmac that defines a typical village road.

The only stop on this trip is to discharge a couple of passengers at the gate of a local major tourist attraction. The other passengers, the two men I had spoken with at the bus stop, chat together. They teasingly make fun of me as we alight at our destination. "We can see that you are going to be enormously helpful!" they chuckle. They had noticed my nodding head and ask "What use are you going to be on the back of the tandem, if you don't have the energy to stay awake on a bus?" I haven't even started my journey yet and I am already receiving the first of the many comments that will be flung at me on this trip, stereotyping the person on the back of a tandem as 'not pulling their weight'!

And there is Nev; waiting.

To be truthful, I am thankful that Nev, being fitter and stronger, had for twenty miles, heroically offered to ride the tandem solo. I had woken that morning, in Scotland, to the sounds of his tinkering with tools. Nev had, in our cramped first-floor bunk-room, for the very first time ever, begun resurrecting the machine which had been dismantled into numerous components to allow optimum packaging for our air travel. Any fault in his workmanship would likely be manifest over those first few miles, so Nev alone would be the recipient of any mechanical disaster or malfunction. More importantly, I could save my energy and avoid any backtracking.

I could begin at John O'Groats, our designated starting point. This also means I have the luxury of having to cycle only forty-six miles, on this, the first day of our adventure.

Nev's face is lit-up with the achievement of his win. His glowing expression is quickly replaced by a veil of concern. "Yeah; but I've done something! Don't know what, but at the moment I can't walk! Maybe pinched a nerve?" he calls, and to prove the intensity of his pain, he is limping cautiously toward me.

Internally my heart is pulsating with an incongruent mix of dread and elation. The thought pops into my head that *'we aren't going to be able to do this trip. In fact, we are not even going to start'*.

"Oh; no! Are you going to be okay?" seems the appropriate response; expressed with the level of sympathy I expect Nev would want to hear in such a dire situation.

What really is important to me though; is that if we were to be unable to complete this journey – at any stage –it will not be because of any inadequacy related to my health, fitness, or lack of ability! Calling the journey quits, because of an injury, would be better if it was incurred by Nev rather than me! I wouldn't be too upset! I have nothing to prove. I would enjoy the time travelling in the UK, no matter what the method of transport! I know though, that Nev, who never ever gives up on anything once he has started, will be frustrated if his expectations of completing this cycling epic are thwarted.

To Nev, pain is a stimulus to be blocked out. 'Pain is weakness leaving the body' he says. It is a phenomenon of the weak that ordinarily, he would never give conscious thought to, let alone speaks of. To see him 'limping', really is cause for concern! My immediate and inappropriate thought, of hiring a car and starting the journey in relative comfort, has to be put aside. I offer sympathetic expressions of encouragement to mask my true feelings!

We wander slowly around this very isolated part of the world that has been incorrectly classified as the most north-eastern point in Scotland! Why is that? We believed that the idea of starting from John O'Groats was because it is the most accessible north-eastern point in Scotland, in fact it is acknowledged as such. Now that we have travelled thousands of kilometres from Australia, we find that, in reality, the most north-eastern part, with a road connection, albeit gravel, is in fact Duncansby Head, and that is another two miles from here! Two miles there and two miles back is a distance just too great to add to today's scheduled itinerary. We quickly dismiss the option to ride to Duncansby Stacks, to see if they are as impressive as the Twelve Apostles – similar rock formations on the southern coast of Victoria, Australia.

The isolation of this part of the world doesn't hold much interest for us. We visit each of the two John O'Groats buildings that are open. The toilet block; I am surprised I have been able to 'hold-on' for this length of time!

Our journey will be guided by the route details that we purchased from the UK National Cycling Charity (CTC). Included with the guide notes was the CTC End to End Record Sheet. We intend to collect an inked stamp to record stopping at each night's destination, and then at the end of the trip we will be entitled to purchase a T-shirt from 'CTC Merchandise', displaying the achievement. We drop into the John O'Groats Souvenir Shop, to receive our first official stamp; confirmation that we have indeed been here; proof of the legitimate start to our journey.

Never having been keen to part with money for 'tourist memorabilia'; we break with tradition and pay to have our photograph taken. A 'pictorial record' of the launch of our endeavour seems obligatory. 'End to End' is the text chosen for the signpost to mark this historic moment in our lives. Even though the distance of 874 miles is also displayed 'ominously' overhead, any apprehension is hidden as we smile broadly while standing astride 'the bike', distanced by the coldness of the steel frame, in correct hierarchical formation. Nev is at the front, ready to 'Captain', and me, in the subordination role of 'Stoker'.

The air is fresh; almost too cool. Our melancholic mood is mirrored in the dullness of the day, which reflects in the gloomy sea. Nev's physical pain has dissolved to mere 'discomfort'. He feels ready to

15

start cycling! This is no fan-fare launch of an exciting adventure. Just two people in 'mid-life', setting out in trepidation, on a tandem ride that they are 'hopeful of accomplishing'

John O'Groats – Armadale

Day One: United Kingdom (UK)
Wednesday, 6th June 2007

Nev has already ridden twenty miles today. My journey has just begun. I appreciate the comfortable start to this expedition. The narrow road is relatively flat, traffic is virtually non-existent and the only weight borne is our own.

Seven miles from John O'Groats we slide past the Castle of Mey. This most northerly inhabited castle on the British mainland had been acquired, at the point of almost abandonment, in 1952, by Her Majesty Queen Elizabeth, the late Queen Mother.

"Nev, I saw a brochure about this castle. The Queen Mother created a garden that is supposed to be well worth visiting. A couple got off the bus here; maybe we should take a look?"

"Well, there's no way we can afford the time on our first day," was the reply I had expected. I craned my neck to try and get a glimpse of the first, 'by-passed attraction', to top my list which I will instead visit via the internet when I return home to Adelaide.

Actually, we had discussed prior to the trip, and agreed, that visits to tourist attractions are going to have to be restricted. Unless the 'site' is directly on the road we are travelling – as is this castle – we will not be able to expend the extra physical energy to make even the smallest detour! Our decision is also based on the sad fact that our memories of previous travels have faded. We cannot recall much of the specifics of buildings, places and tourist destinations, that we visited during the travels we took through the United Kingdom and Europe, thirty-two years ago. Our brain cells were young then, so how much more limited capacity would we have now to remember these brief momentary encounters on this venture?

Thurso is our designated lunch stop and we return to our hostel there. Nev shows me the Redback spider that must have inhabited the bike's cardboard carton while it had been stored in our garage at home. The 'stow-away' must have crawled from the bike box to become acquainted with these new Scottish climes. It is now stuck to the windowsill, glued by its dried out innards, red-back still intact. Nev had squashed it to prevent a 'northern hemisphere infestation'. We eat, gather our gear and securely fix to the tandem, the loaded panniers. Items that need to be easily accessible: camera, passports, money, PDA, maps, fills the handle-bar bag. Other travel paraphernalia such as lunch bag, raincoats and any items that cannot be squeezed into one of the four 'panniers', are strapped by 'bungee cords' to the front and rear carriers. Nev had brought a tarpaulin along, thinking it might come in handy to wrap the tandem in. He decides now that this would not after all be sufficient to hide the tandem from any officious train conductor on our future train travels, so it is 'donated' to the hostel.

The only way to complete this trip is to get started. I have already decided that the best way to approach the journey, in a positive way, is to cope with one hour at a time. If I achieve that successfully, I will surely be able to double that hour and thereby complete two hours and so on! If I can complete the first day, I will then take one day at a time!

I remember applying this approach to my marriage. Not that I had taken on marriage as a force to be reckoned with, rather more on a scale of wanting to fulfil the 'forever' vow. At the time of our marriage I had been employed as a clerk at the New Zealand Department of Social Welfare. My role was to approve the 'Domestic Purposes Benefit' to women who had, through a variety of circumstances, found themselves living alone with dependent children to support, and no longer with their husbands income – no such thing as 'partners' back then! As a nineteen year old I had listened to the anguish brought about by 'split custody' and 'split possessions'. At that young age I became adamant that I would never, in my life, be in that situation.

For me, the first year of marriage – at the same young age - had passed quickly and had not been at all onerous; after all we were still in the honeymoon phase as a couple, living in London and enjoying independence from our families. It was easy at that point in our relationship to be sure that I would get enjoyment from our relationship for another year. Each anniversary I had doubled the length this marriage was going to be successful. I stopped applying this philosophy after having accomplished about fifteen years. To double at that point was too look too far into the future!

Our fifteenth anniversary was also the time that life's focus was on raising two pre-school age children. I don't remember applying this strategy when my children were born. Maybe by then I had stopped romanticising, or had accepted the inevitable permanence of those dependent milestones! To date our marriage has exceeded double those fifteen years. Surely, I thought, the relationship is still healthy if we are embarking on this epic journey together?

Travelling on the bike, fully laden, is a new experience. The tandem, built in the USA, had been delivered by airmail, to our doorstep in Australia, just four weeks before our departure for Britain! We'd had a few practise runs to see if we could actually ride 'the thing', but we hadn't had the opportunity to test the weight or the balance of a load. The nearest replication we had achieved was a ride of a couple of hours along Adelaide's 'Linear Park'. With clay bricks evenly balanced in the panniers, our trial load was a serious underestimation of what the actual ride would finally feel like. Today is to be a day of settling in to a rhythm that we can both find comfortable!

Although the breeze contributes coolness, the afternoon is clear and sun-filled. The scenery along the north coast of Scotland is stunning. We often have the North Sea in view and the green pastures are still lush with spring growth. Fields are dotted with highland cattle, thick shaggy coats testimony to the harshness of the local winters.

To our right the symmetry of the cluster of energy-generating wind-turbines is a brief reminder that we live in the 21st Century. Each tower generates enough energy to power about 6000 homes. The engineered elegance seems odd, standing tall in fields bounded by dry-stone walled fences. Walls built when candlelight and lanterns would have been the only lighting source and built to enclose sheep, rather than farms of sustainable energy.

Later the vista is scarred by an imposing conglomeration of abandoned buildings. Dounreay Nuclear Power Development Establishment was closed because of a decline in demand for the extracted uranium and plutonium, from spent nuclear fuel, that was reprocessed there. As a New Zealand national I am reminded of the 'No Nuke' slogans of the late 80's.

Born in 1956 my formative years were exposed to discussions and media publications on the opposition, from the mid 1960's, to French nuclear testing on Mururoa Atoll in the Pacific. The New Zealand and Australian governments took France to the International Court of Justice in an attempt to ban their testing. Greenpeace, often operating from New Zealand, was a significant opposing force and Greenpeace vessels, protesting against nuclear testing, sailed into the test site in 1972, and in 1973.

My children would probably believe that the reality of modern terrorism was born of the September 11, 2001 Twin Towers destruction. For me, the earliest act of terrorism, although the media never named it as such, that left a lasting impression on me, was the sinking, in 1985, of the Greenpeace flagship Rainbow Warrior. The Rainbow Warrior had been involved in the Pacific protests. It was moored in Auckland, New Zealand, when agents of the French Secret Service blew it up to prevent it leaving for another protest campaign. A Portuguese crew member, Fernando Pereira, was killed in the explosions.

While the attack had been on the international organisation Greenpeace, we New Zealanders took it as a personal attack on us, as it was carried out on our soil. Relationships between France and New Zealand seriously deteriorated for a period. The French threatened New Zealand's access to the important European Economic Community market. New Zealand exports to France were boycotted. New Zealand retaliated in boycotting French imports.

The New Zealand government positioned itself as world leader of the anti-nuclear movement, when it made a decision to ban visits by nuclear propelled or armed ships, from its waters. The law was controversial at the time as it effectively severed the ANZUS defence treaty and consequently caused a rift in relations with the United States. The 20th anniversary of that event was to be in two days, on June 8th, 2007.

That government decision, with public support, to regard nuclear as a potential stimulus for environmental and social decimation, and to ban nuclear resources in New Zealand, has influenced my personal view about all things nuclear. In my adopted country, Australia, there has been much recent debate about nuclear energy versus coal-fired power stations, or the alternative environmentally friendlier, solar and wind generated options. While there is strong political support for nuclear to be the provider of energy in the future; I have an inherent fear of the world facing a catastrophe brought about by nuclear malfunction so my personal preference favours environmentally friendly solutions.

It is great for Nev and I to be able to chat easily to each other. My only contribution to the decision about what equipment we should bring for this trip had been influenced by an American article that I had read on the Internet. While captaining a tandem with his wife as 'stoker', this guy had occasion to call to her "Whoa!" and she had thought he said "go!" So she responded by 'digging-in' when he wanted her to 'ease off'.   He   was   therefore   now   promoting   the communicative advantage of an intercom system between captain and stoker. I insisted that we have one. So Nev now carries the system in his back pocket. A thin wire goes from the control box, up his back beneath his cycle-top, to the headset he wears. Another wire crosses the gap between us, to my headset. This gives us much the same opportunity to converse as if we were sitting beside each other in a car. We can have normal conversation – with background music if we choose - at a volume that is easily heard, rather than just minimal communication via shouted and possibly misunderstood instructions.

This British icon appeared in the middle of no-where

Roads   following   coastlines   characteristically climb up and over headlands. This afternoon's ride doesn't deviate from this theme. We fall into a rhythm that is not so much natural, but rather the product of previous arguments, tears (mine), and frustration experienced by both of us.

Nev has had twenty years of mountain bike racing experience. His greatest result was to be placed 9th in the world while representing New Zealand in the 'Veteran grade' at the 1996 World Mountain Bike Championships in Cairns, Australia. He had also been selected to represent New Zealand in that grade in Vail, Colorado in 1994, and on that occasion had finished mid-field. Nev continues to race mountain bikes in the Super Masters grade at local and National level. Super Masters is the grade name for participants over fifty years, but in Nev's case the name is equally applicable to 'superbly mastering' a passionate past-time. While my riding prowess is by no means at novice level; I now only occasionally ride for social recreation. As such, my ability is infinitely inferior. For the success of this 'coupling' we have to operate at the same level.

Our practices had shown that Nev had no option but to bring down his superior strength and skill to my level. The frustration he expressed showed how excruciatingly difficult this was for him. I overheard Nev telling his mates "I'll be teaching Lou a thing or two about cadence, and I reckon that having to follow my technique will be one of the benefits of the trip for her." To date though, I know he has found me a slow learner. Besides, I find Nev doesn't practice what he preaches! He explained the importance of rotating the pedals at about ninety-five revolutions a minute. Oddly, though I was weaker and should have benefited from his experience and wisdom, I found this caused my spring-loaded seat-support to get a 'bounce on', and the pace felt as frenetic as the spinning legs of the Road Runner cartoon character, and far from energy conserving! By contrast when we started climbing a steep hill - the very time that I would, on my own bike, have dropped the gears down to spin freely - Nev would be slogging upward; with me begging for mercy!

In the initial stages of our learning, I had been convinced that we could never get this 'twosome' in unison. I had cried tears of frustration!

Nev tried to reassure me. "I'm not doing this deliberately. I don't want to jeopardise our trip. We have no choice but to work together."

"What if I can't make it" was my tearful reply.

"Don't worry, we'll find an alternative – take a train or something if we absolutely have to. We'll easily manage the distances and you'll have time to rest each day. We will make it work!" Nev reassured me.

Female genetics, less opportunity to have developed a history of prowess (I had just finished raising a family to their completion of high school, as well as working part-time), and to some extent a lesser interest in sport, meant it was impossible for me to quickly develop additional muscle or fitness to rise to even a little of Nev's strength and ability. The compromise had to rest with him! Nev quickly became attuned to when I, as the 'auxiliary engine', wasn't performing. The load would become largely his and he would change-down to a level that I could manage, before I could nag in his ear with "Have you got another gear?" No man appreciates a wife who is a 'back seat driver'!

Climbing up and over a headland, pedalling easily down the other side, just to climb again, becomes the steady repetition of the afternoon. We have just topped a particularly long, steep gradient that has left my legs feeling like 'lead balloons' and my chest taut.

The descent we are about to enjoy' only precedes another climb, which, from this vantage, looks harder, higher and longer, than any other that we have climbed today.

We must be getting close to our destination so we stop to orientate ourselves to the map. Peering into the distance we are both pleased to notice a signpost directing right, at the base of our imminent descent. We figure that will be the direction we will take to our destination, Armadale. That's a relief! Clearly though, the long climb will be our first challenge tomorrow.

It is already starting to feel cool when we finally locate the 'Old School House'. We are warmly welcomed by the owner as we prop the tandem against the stone of the school room wall. The adjoining school house is his home; we will stay for the night in the old school which has been converted into holiday accommodation. We are the first tenants of the summer season.

Day One Stats:

Nev's cycle computer records kilometres so includes his solo journey from Thurso to John O'Groats.

Distance covered: 105 kilometres

My Speedo is recording a running tally of miles: 47.79 miles covered today from John O'Groats to Armadale

Reminiscing

The bath is sheer luxury. I haven't had a bath for years! Short showers are the ablution of necessity in water-scarce Adelaide. Soaking away the difficulties of the last few days and immersing in the surrealism of total exhaustion, my thoughts drift as haphazardly as they had been while we have been cycling.

Our reintroduction to England had been disappointing. Heathrow Airport was aesthetically tired, the carpet threadbare; probably the same carpet we had trod on last time we arrived 33 years ago! Certainly the tube that took us to Kings Cross appeared to be the very one, new in 1973, that had transported us all those years ago to London's city sights. The deepest Piccadilly line delivered us to 'King's Cross Station'. With no lift or escalator in sight, the only way to resurface was via the stairs. We were weary from our flights and had our first, and during this trip, often to be repeated, physically demanding experience of lugging our gear. Nev would hoist the boxed tandem to one landing, scoot back down to me and help me lug our various bags before he would repeat the process to the next landing. I felt sorry for the people, older than us, who were struggling to haul their heavy suitcases, bumping them upwards, step by step. The mother country has become haggard and demented with age, whilst the colonies of New Zealand and Australia have embraced Occupational Health and Safety regulations, in an effort to ward off liability claims. It was clear that the Olympics in 2012 were going to drag London into the 21st Century — signs displaying impending redevelopment, indicated that this was going to be so.

Our first visit to London had been as young newly weds in November 1975. We had arrived fresh from a lifetime of living with our families in Palmerston North, a rural New Zealand city, and had found central London fast-paced and grand. London had been our home for two winters. The first winter we lived in a small bedsit at 21 Sutton Court Road, Chiswick.

My work at the Heinz factory was in a job that I had obtained under false pretences. I had no knowledge of factory work, as my occupation had been clerical. Nev though, had a high school holiday job at Prepared Foods (the workplace of his mother and step-father) in Palmerston North. He described what his role had been — mostly making cardboard templates into boxes, filling empty jars with pickled onions, and lugging pallets loaded with canned goods. I went along for the interview at Heinz with this assumed knowledge. I was able to bluff my way into securing a job, which incidentally had little relevance to my untruthful New Zealand experience. Nev had worked in an industry that was canning by hand, whereas Heinz was fully automated. Quick to learn, I was able to master a variety of tasks from machine operation to quality control, related to the canning of baked beans.

Nev got work as a builder's labourer, restoring an historic building; the original market building adjoining the Tabard Hotel in Turnham Green. The second winter we lived, again, in a one roomed bedsit, at 11 Montrose Place, Queens Park.   We both succeeded in getting work at the Heinz factory.   Nev was happy to have indoor work for the winter season.

We had frugally 'squirreled away' most of what we earned for future travel, the first summer to Europe and the second summer travelling towards home, New Zealand, via America.   Even though we lived on an extremely tight budget, the theatre seats 'up in the gods', visits to historic buildings and museums, browsing grand palaces and department stores like Selfridges and Harrods, had all made living in London sophisticated and exciting.

"Where has London gone?"   I exclaimed when we surfaced from the underground.   The years of absence had, built in my mind, a London of towering buildings that now, in reality, had paled to insignificance when compared to the high-rises of southern hemisphere cities, where we had transited; such as Bangkok and Singapore.

As our arrival time in London was late evening, and we were departing by train early the next morning, the accommodation we had chosen on the Internet, was because of its proximity to King's Cross station. The Jesmond Dene Hotel was a mere 150 metre trundle.

It was 9 p.m. and we were beginning to feel jaded and sleep deprived as we walked into the Hotel foyer.   When the hotel receptionist explained, in her strong Eastern European accent, "Sorry there has been a mistake. You are actually booked at our 'sister-hotel'. It's only a short distance away."   Our faces clearly reflected the annoyance we felt. This meant trundling somewhere else with our load of luggage – something we had clearly tried to avoid. The receptionist decided to double-check and then thankfully confirmed, via a phone call to the other establishment, that she had "incorrectly informed us." So we were pleased to be able to stay where we stood after all. Pleased that is, until we were shown the poky room that was up a short twist of stairs, and then the shared bathroom that was back down two flights and then told that breakfast, which was included, was not served until 8 o'clock.

"But we have to catch a train at 7.30 a.m., surely that is a late hour to serve breakfast when people are travelling?" Nev questioned.

The receptionist offered to bring some food to our room this evening, so that we could then eat breakfast in the morning at our convenience. Her knock at the door, probably only moments after we had arrived in our room, woke us. On opening the door, she passed me a small plate, on which were two, uncovered, slices of white bread and miniature containers of butter and jam. These I carried in a sleep-walking state to the mantelpiece. When next I saw these morsels the following morning, they were dry, brittle and curled at the edges. London was only yesterday morning, a surreal thirty-six hours ago!

Most travellers start this epic journey from the south; hence it is commonly referred to as LEJOG (Lands End to John O'Groats, from Cornwall to Scotland). We had gambled with the possibility of meeting head winds at times and had chosen to travel from north to south, starting from Scotland. For us the acronym JOGLE (John O'Groats to Lands End) is more appropriate. One of the main reasons that we chose to travel in a southerly direction, Scotland to Cornwall, was that it will allow us one day of 'relaxation' before we begin our adventure. The prospect of expending energy - riding on the tandem - when our bodies and brains were still in the southern hemisphere time-zone and wanting to sleep, hadn't been appealing. The decision to travel from London to Thurso, all day by train, was to give us the opportunity to 'doze' if we needed, and time to adjust to the new meridian.

Travelling north from London by train, the terrain had looked relatively flat or 'rolling' countryside. The outlook was beginning to instil in me a quiet confidence that this was not, as Nev had promised, going to be too difficult. Even the highlands north of Edinburgh were soothed by the fading light that softened the skyward outline. The frolicking of deer and rabbits amongst the grasses beside the railway, created an atmosphere of ease that was further muted by the dusk.

Another reason that we started from Scotland was, from what Nev had researched on the 'Net', travelling by train with a tandem had complications. He figured that with the bike still boxed from the plane trip, its true identity would be disguised. I had overheard Nev explain to a friend; "I'm not worried; I'm always ready for a challenge."

'How much of a challenge could this mode of transport be?' I wondered. *'What wasn't he telling me?'*

Nev had constructed the cardboard box out of one complete bike carton, with an extension achieved by cutting up part of a second carton. This created the 1.9 metre casing. Including the extra tools, helmets, carriers, and spare parts stowed with the bike, the entire packaged weight of thirty kilograms was too heavy and awkward to carry. To move this weighty item of luggage, an old suitcase trolley was securely attached by a bungee cord to one end of the carton. Nev could now lift and pull from the opposite end to the suitcase trolley, and the simple contraption would be perambulated along. Incidentally those thirty kilograms also exceeded the twenty-five kilograms flight baggage allocation, but was resolved when the check-in officer assigned five kilos to my significantly lighter load.

Whenever we were 'on foot', during our journey, all of the remaining baggage was my responsibility. My body was the means of carriage (and support) of the load of luggage. I had a light day-pack on my back. In my left hand I carried two large, fully loaded panniers, clasped together by their straps. Two smaller panniers also crammed full, and a thermal lunch bag, were secure within a zip-topped, red and blue striped bag – the sort that you pick up from 'bargain shops' for $2, this I carried in my right hand. The straps of the striped bag on the right were a little longer than those on the left hand. The burden stretched my arms to tendon snapping capacity. I shuffled along like a Japanese lady, tottering with my uneven load, trying to stay balanced, and desperate to 'keep up'.

Nev is small of stature with strong, short legs, that 'propel' rather than 'stroll'. There is only ever one pace for his mobility, and that is 'flat-out'. I was relieved that now, as we had commenced cycling, for the next sixteen days, my carrying job would be virtually redundant. The gear was now securely attached to the tandem!

We had been in England for only twelve hours when Nev was faced with his first train challenge. Train reservations had been 'made' from Australia, but not easily. Nev had experienced difficulties while attempting to make an on-line train booking that included the bike, so he had resorted to phoning the British Rail call centre – probably based in India! On arriving at Kings Cross we had to collect our tickets for our travel the following day. This was duly achieved through presentation of our booking details at the ticket office. At the point of boarding the train though, Nev was stopped by a ticket inspector who wanted to see the train ticket for the bike. This we had not received, and we had no idea that a ticket was required. We logically thought that, having made a booking - to include the bike, we would have been given everything necessary to sufficiently fulfil the requirements of the travel process. The inspector explained that there was space for four bikes in the designated 'cycle-carriage' and if that space was not fully taken we would be able to 'board' with our boxed-bike. Fortunately there was only one other cycle in the allocated space. This meant that we could leave Kings Cross, but we were warned it did not necessarily guarantee a smooth transition later, when we changed trains at Edinburgh.

On the outskirts of Edinburgh the train we were travelling on had been halted. The train was standing motionless on the tracks. We were worrying about whether we were going to miss our connection, while a potential suicider was being cajoled to 'get down' from one of the overbridges and not end their life squashed on the tracks. I'm not sure what decision the person made but eventually we began rolling slowly into Edinburgh, fortunately arriving just in time to transition to the Thurso train. It turned out that we had no difficulty stowing the bike after all.

The train bound for Thurso rocked and clacked rhythmically, lulling my jetlagged brain into reverie. Why do people make this journey? Our native land is New Zealand and from the northern North Island, Cape Reinga, to southern North Island, Wellington, is 1096 km, (680 miles) of very picturesque scenery. Although less distance than this (John O'Groats to Lands End trip is about 890 miles) I have never heard of anyone, let alone thousands each year, wanting to complete the New Zealand journey.

Edinburgh Station, Scotland; our luggage and packaged tandem, with the improvised trolley

Apparently it all began with a Cornishman, who walked to John O'Groats in 1879 with a wheelbarrow, presumably to carry his suitcase! Back in those days the media was nowhere near as far reaching as it is now, so how the world became aware of this journey, and why people want to follow in the footsteps of a Cornishman, is a mystery, especially as most travellers start in civilized Cornwall and finish the 'End to End' trip in the isolation of Scotland! For whatever reason, it has become the ultimate UK journey, travelled in either direction, by foot, or every type of wheeled transport imaginable.

In spite of Nev enjoying the challenge of a race, we are not out to break any records. Our sixteen day journey will be at a leisurely pace as we have already been well and truly defeated by the fastest ever time for a 'mixed tandem couple'. They completed the distance in an incredible, two days and three hours!

Armadale – Carbisdale Castle

Day Two: UK
Thursday, 7th June

I'm buried under a weight of quilts and doze through memories of recent winter snugness. The deepest ten hours of sleep, drifts into a new sunlit morning and I have to remind myself that it is actually summer now, and I am in Scotland.

We relax over a meagre breakfast of cheese-on-toast. Apart from our emergency freeze-dried 'rations', the meal depletes the only food we carry. While we were home in Adelaide, it had concerned me that getting enough food may be a problem. I expected we would be eating an enormous amount to replace the 'burned' calories and had jokingly suggested we make our trip into a Reality-TV program. This would have meant bringing along a video camera to record the agony and the ecstasy of the trip. I thought we could, at the end of each day's ride, video ourselves approaching an unsuspecting couple in a village street. We would then encourage them to take us to their home, give us a hearty meal and a bed for the night. Maybe a great idea, but we didn't have enough confidence, or time, to turn the idea into a reality.

The panniers are packed and hitched to our 'trusty steed' and we are ready to go. In the advice I had received about control of continence, about twenty minutes after consumption of breakfast, I am supposed to go and sit quietly for ten minutes to achieve a 'motion'. I have been informed by 'experts' eliminating my, almost always, state of constipation may resolve the irritation that I experience with my bladder. I give the advice some cursory thought but decide there is no way that I can initiate such a considerable delay to the start of our ride each morning. I have, up until very recently, deliberately kept my problems from Nev and I am now reluctant to have him affected by the possible solution! I reckon it would be impossible for me to 'relax' when I know that Nev is 'champing at the bit' to leave, so I decide that I will focus on this remedy when I return home to Adelaide.

Today Nev is already trying to convince me to divert from the agreed route choice we had set in the comfort of our 'home office' in Adelaide. He found a stack of tourist pamphlets on a shelf beside the stairs as he made his way up to bed last night. One brochure presents an alternative route to the UK Cycle Touring Club one that we plan to follow. I am reluctant to deviate from such a well-planned and much travelled route. We decide to make our way to Bettyhill where we will get some food and the benefit of local knowledge, before we finally commit to the route choice.

A gentle downhill cruise drops us quickly to rejoin the main road, hang a right, and 'cold turkey' straight up the hill. It's a challenge. My body is not yet 'warmed up'. I'm trying to relax. This 'stoking' role is not second nature. *'I must do as instructed in the manual'.* I focus on keeping my weight centrally balanced. *'Try not to lean. This seat is really not comfortable; I'm thirsty; already! Try not to jiggle! I need to go to the toilet; already! Concentrate on not pedalling too hard, keep those pedals rotating in circles.'* Pedals turning in circles is something that seems obvious, as all pedals are connected to a shaft and subsequently to a round sprocket that logically only turns in a circle. Pushing down on the pedals is not the ideal style. *'The day has hardly started. You've got a long way to go'.* The whirlwind of thoughts fill my head. And we climb over the 'brow' to arrive in Bettyhill.

"Wow that was some hill; four miles!" I gasp.

We come across one very small shop with signage displaying that it is 'Licensed to sell groceries'. From within we select an assortment of food, and the locals confirm that a change of decision, to 'go down the Strath' will be a better option for us. Our initial choice, to Tongue, would have been over the 'high road', similar terrain to that which we have covered to this point. A continuation of highs and lows, with some long climbs, doesn't appeal right now.

The first 'historic marker' is at the bridge. I reach to pull the tourist brochure from my back pocket. I have it now and am turning to the first page as we cross. Wind whips up unexpectedly and the brochure is torn from my grasp! I want to stop and retrieve it. I want to stop right now. In a split instinctive reaction I put the brakes on. Only problem is, I don't have any. I just, with force, stop pedalling. Now Nev is in full circular mode to gain forward momentum, oblivious to what I am trying to achieve behind!

"Whoa, I've dropped it! I need to get the guide before it blows off the bridge."

The clash and mash of confused pedal strokes draws the bike to a stop. I run to capture the paper from the playful breeze and we're off again.

That was interesting! I do have a semblance of control after all. This important discovery, that I could initiate stopping, was something that I was able to put to good use, but in a gentler fashion, at times over the coming days.

The route we decide on meanders seventeen miles south from Bettyhill through the long, wide valley of Strathnaver. The single-track B road follows the Naver River at first and then along Loch Naver to Altnaharra.

What a pretty day this is. The sun gently warming, and the rippling river and verdant whispering grasses are a stunning foreground to the highland backdrop. This is 'picture-perfect' countryside, dotted with quaint stone crofts, framed by dry-stone walls. Arched stone bridges cross the myriad of streams. What a wonderful feeling to be moving parallel with the earth instead of pushing skyward up the hills!

The region is heavy with the history of 'the clearings' of the early 1800's. The area had to be cleared of the subsistence crofters in residence at that time, as a decision had been made to increase the income from the land by letting it to sheep farmers. The Highlanders, some 15,000, were forced from the 1.5 million acre estate of the Duke of Stafford (later made the Duke of Sutherland). There was little notice given and the crofters fled to the coast to escape the flames burning the land and their homes. The action was viewed by some of the instigators of the 'clearing' as putting the barbarous Highlanders into a better position, where they could associate together and apply themselves to industry, educate their children, and advance in civilization.

It strikes me that too often history is just a record of who was more powerful than whom at any particular point in civilisation. Sparked by a greater desire, by the party that considered itself more superior, for wealth from land, diamonds, gold, oil or whatever resource is coveted. Many desires have been 'acquired' and the displacement of natives justified, through the misguided intent to improve the natives' lives.

We stop for a snack and sit to eat on the dry-stone wall fronting the Altnaharra hotel. To this point we have seen only one vehicle, so find it amusing when a little 'Postman Pat' postal van zooms past. We chuckle again when another goes by in the opposite direction, about ten minutes later.

Back on the bike I have too much time to think. My bladder problems are taking precedence and the thoughts are not positive! It happens like this. I can be happily cycling along with no desire at all to urinate, yet when we stop to take a photo, or for some other reason, the instant I dismount from the bike I have the most intensely urgent need to 'go'. This sensation is unexpected and ridiculous, and I squeeze every muscle I have to maintain my composure. Sometimes I find it is best to fold my upper body and whilst bent double, with fists tightly clenched around the top bar of the bike and with legs crossed, I get my bladder to change its mind. This is very irritating and also a painfully embarrassing antic to secure control, at least for as long as it takes for me to leap behind the privacy offered by a stone fence! I am thankful that Nev just waits patiently for me. I would dearly like to know what is causing this problem.

Have I damaged my sphincter from too much time on a bike seat, am I sipping so much water that 'the balloon is about to burst', or is it because I have been seated and warm and there is a rush of cool air to the nether regions, or have I just completely lost it as I enter my dotage? Whatever the reason, it is a dilemma that I must control, as I do not want to spend my days cycling in mawkish wet padded cycling pants. I think you get the unpleasant picture, and so I am not going to mention this problem again, other than to say that it continued to plague me for the length of this trip and beyond!

The steps of Syre Church of Scotland are chosen as our lunch-break seating. The small church was built in the late 19th century. Its white painted exterior walls are of corrugated iron. The door is open and a little porch invites us to view the church interior. Soft natural light from the square and diamond shaped leadlight panels that glaze the three windows on each side; show plainly decorated white wood panelling and half a dozen rows of wooden pews. Services are conducted at 3 p.m. every 2nd, 4th and 5th Sunday.

Following lunch Nev suggests that I take the helm. The flat narrow road is an ideal opportunity for me to see if I can manage the weight of the tandem and also to give my backside some reprieve. Nev knows that I have found the back seat difficult to 'meld' with. Our very first ride back in Australia had, for my 'sit-bones', been extremely uncomfortable. This had been quite frustrating because Nev had chosen a superior brand of seat on the recommendation of a number of reports. So after only twenty-four hours of ownership and twenty-four kilometres of riding, we were at our local bike-shop looking for a more comfortable saddle for me.

I knew I was going to have to sit on the seat for about one hundred and fifty hours during the trip, yet I had to make a decision about what saddle to purchase after riding only 500 meters around a city block. We did this three times, each circuit testing a different brand of seat! I chose the best, of a not so comfortable bunch, and left the shop with a feeling that I had been quite hard to please. I have managed to soften the pressure by tucking the 'rigidity' under a blanket of cosy grey wool. My long-fleece, sheepskin seat cover, was a secretive last minute internet purchase, by me, from a New Zealand supplier. Knowing Nev, I am not surprised that he despises the cover. I suspected trailing a fluffy seat would not fit with his sense of what is appropriate equipment for a venture of athleticism!

The position in the 'Captain's' seat is more upright. I really do feel like a Captain, although not of a ship. From this vantage point I feel more like I am driving a heavy, fully loaded Mack truck. Nev is not being a relaxed 'stoker' having never mastered the personal discipline required to be a subordinate! I reckon I can feel his tension through the frame. The slightest movement of the handlebars threatens to swerve us dangerously. Pins and needles 'tingle' in my left hand. I must be gripping the handlebars too tightly. In spite of Nev's wriggling, the dependence on me to keep the tandem upright and moving forward is paramount. I must keep this machine controlled. After thirty minutes the responsibility becomes overwhelming. I am happy to pass the helm back to 'Captain' Nev. An ice-cream treat at the campground store, beside the stunningly beautiful Loch Naver, is a suitable time to swap.

At the intersection where we rejoin the main road of Scotland, we glance behind to look towards the hills in the North, and take pleasure in our good fortune at finding the 'Strathnaver Trail brochure', and the relatively flat valley route.

The single-lane main road, with passing bays every 500 metres, is indicative of the small amount of traffic in this area. We make a game of moving as quickly as we can to the next passing bay whenever we become aware of a vehicle approaching from behind. The game was born of the disconcertion we felt when one particular vehicle hovered on our rear, and we could feel the impatience of the driver over the lack of opportunity to pass easily.

One of the few times I took the lead in the Captain's position. Going down 'the Strath'.

The route continues south through forested areas and then alongside Loch Shin to Lairg, and beyond.

I nudge Nev's shoulder. "Look over there, out to the right, that's magnificent!" Standing grandly on the other side of the river a beautiful castle, turrets and towers surrounded by trees, has come into view. I am so excited to find that this impressive structure is in fact Carbisdale Castle, our destination for the night. What a wonderful way to end a perfect day. We talk of hot showers and massages to revive our weary muscles.

The guide notes indicate we can overcome the obstacle of the Kyle River that flows between us and the castle, by taking a shortcut across a nearby railway bridge. This will enable us to avoid continuing several extra miles south by road to Bonar Bridge, and then doubling back to the castle. Of course we choose to take the railway bridge option. There is a footpath, a shorter distance; the choice is obvious.

Veering onto the lane-like road to our left, a sharp climb leads to the full-height of the railway bridge; the extra effort confirming the weariness in our legs. A few steps lead up to a barricade. We are now confronted with an obstacle; the solid bar has to be crossed to gain access to the bridge footpath. This would be such a simple endeavour for people 'on foot'. Our heavily laden, rigid mule, (which is 2 ½ meters long), bucks at the barrier; presenting us with no option but to unburden 'the beast'. We unload all of the panniers. With our best strongman skills we then hoist the tandem over the barricade. The four panniers are refitted and we make our way across the bridge, only to repeat the process again, so that we can exit the footpath at the other end!

The impressive gate-post to Carbisdale Castle is a welcome end to a long day. As we wind our way up the driveway, there before us is a sight that will make this day even more perfect. A short distance in front, a couple, riding abreast on separate bikes, struggle up the driveway. Our competitiveness comes to the fore. We are now in a race, and at this particular point, we are the losers. How tragic are we, to put in effort and pass in brilliant form, and then thrill to the win, just in the nick of time, as we pull up beside the castle door?

The grand foyer is dominated by an enormous ornate fireplace, empty now, but what a wonderful welcome the warmth must have been in times past. We have arrived at what surely must be the world's most impressive Youth Hostel! At check-in we are given directions to our separate dormitories. Dormitory! Separate! How can that be? The receptionist was in fact providing exactly what we had booked. We had forgotten that at the time of our internet search for accommodation, no double rooms had been available here. The experience of staying one night in a castle had been an opportunity we had not wanted to miss. Oh well, for tonight, put aside any romantic notions and cancel the massage!

I make my way to the 'ladies dormitory' nestled on the top floor. After showering I meet with Nev to explore the grand rooms, spread over three levels. Rich burgundy walls hold enormous portraits in oil, framed in heavy gilt filigree. Elegant white Italian marble statuary decorates the centre of the main hallway and wall niches.

The castle was built for Mary Mitchell a colourful character, according to articles recording the castle history. It seems to me that there was also the slightest hint in the writings, that skulduggery was possibly also part of Mary's character. Mary had lost her first husband in a shooting accident at a hunt. On her second marriage to George Granville William Sutherland Levenson-Gower, 3rd Duke and 18th Earl of Sutherland, Mary became Duchess of Sutherland. Mary was not popular with the Sutherland family and when the Earl died, and left almost his entire estate to Mary, who had been his wife for only three years, his son and heir contested the will. Mary destroyed documents relating to the hearing and for these actions ended up in prison for six weeks! Eventually, as part of the financial settlement, it was agreed the family would build the Duchess a home, in keeping with her station, at their expense and to her specifications, so long as it was outside the Sutherland lands. Hence this beautiful castle was built during the years from 1906-1917.

Carbisdale Castle, near Bonar Bridge, Scotland

Mary remarried, and Carbisdale was brought in 1933, by Colonel Theodore Salvesen, a wealthy Scottish businessman of Norwegian decent. After Colonel Salvesen's death his son Captain Harold Salvesen inherited the castle. I am thankful that in 1945 he gifted the castle, contents and estate to the Scottish Youth Hostel Association, so that travellers like us could enjoy the unique experience of staying in a castle.

The dining room serves a three course meal for £8. The brim-full bowl of mushroom soup is thick and creamy, the most delicious I have ever tasted. This is followed by an enormous portion of Fish Mornay that threatens to overflow from the plate. A large slice of the British Banoffee Pie is served as the sweet course. Made of pastry, cream, bananas and caramelised condensed milk this rich and delectable dessert is a struggle for me to consume. I have over indulged! Fully sated I have no choice but to seek the comfort that comes with being horizontal. I take myself to my top-bunk, lie down with the friendship of a good novel and hope those calories I have just consumed, move to the areas of my body that will need their sustenance. Mileage similar to that covered today will be faced again tomorrow!

Day Two Stats:

Distance covered 99.21 kilometres, 61.64 miles

Nev's cycle computer records our average speed at 20.5 kph.

Ride time: 4 hours 50 minutes.

My Speedo is keeping a tally of the total miles of the trip - 109.43 miles to date.

Carbisdale Castle - Loch Ness

Day Three: UK
Friday, 8th June

I am dreading this day, as we are expecting to ride a distance of sixty miles, and also because all the books I have read about cycle touring warn that the third day will be the most difficult! I don't know whether I should expect to have to push through a physical pain barrier, or whether hormonal blues, similar to those following childbirth, will be the setback. I had, many years ago, experienced a slight 'baby-blues' hormonal despondency, so was prepared for an 'emotionally unstable' day.

The enormous breakfast is a positive start. Individual trays have been set with cereal, juice, yoghurt and fruit and there is any area in the dining room where toast can be made. I eat as much as my stomach can hold, and still have enough of my ration left over to bring with me for morning tea.

It's not long before we are into a long steady climb. The road is hugging the edge of the valley cut by the Kyle River deep below. Cool morning mist envelopes us as the gradient steepens. I try to focus on the scenery. There is a cliff-like bank on our right and to our left tree tops, parallel to the road, spring from unseen depths beside the river. I've habitually been a bit of a worrier, and definitely an over-thinker, so am used to having a brain that doesn't easily switch-off. Right now I have, *'one misty moisty morning when cloudy was the weather'*, repetitively jingling through my head. Over and over, only that one line from the children's nursery rhyme 'sings with a tempo' to match each pedal rotation. The repetitive ditty is neither calming nor distracting and the tune is not loud enough to drown out the screaming of my legs. I give their pain voice and yell the discomfort of their effort at Nev.

"Give me another gear, man!" A few pedal strokes later, "I need another one," and then again "have you got any more?" I puff out these demands between large intakes of breath.

"Well I reckon I'm going to have to use 'granny' now, I have been hoping not to have to" he responds calmly.

I splutter in disbelief, "Do you mean to tell me that on all the hills, over the past two days, when I have been begging for more (gears that is) you have been holding out on me?"

'Granny' is not in this sense named because of achievement through one's children's procreation, although I am in age qualified for the position, and already achieved, three-fold, by my younger sister! 'Granny' is the lowest gear on the bike; number twenty seven. I love 'granny' – she has enough teeth to bite into any challenge (twenty-four teeth on the front sprocket and thirty-two on the rear). I know though that Nev, with his superior leg strength, avoids 'getting into granny'. It would be so 'not macho', to ever confess to assistance from 'Granny', even for the weariest of legs or to top the most difficult climb. And so Nev now humbly succumbs to my demands, and with 'granny's' help we climb the 660 feet to the bleakness atop Struie Hill, where we are presented with a cool, 360 degree' misted panorama.

Large lilac blooms, of the azaleas that are growing wild, beautify the roadside verges. Lush farmland is interrupted periodically by villages, quaint with stone terraced houses, neatly tended gardens and stone churches. Such quiet little communities remind me of the retirement village where I work in Adelaide. Do young people live and work in these quiet, isolated little places? Culrain, Ardgay, Culcairn, Evanton, following Cromarty Firth to Dingwall, then inland to Muir of Ord. It's comforting to notice that these villages nestle beside the railway, so if we do need to bale out, we have an alternative!

Traffic begins to thicken as we are almost at Drumnadrochit, the centre of the 'Loch Ness industry' in Scotland. Numerous vehicles overtake, so much so that I feel intimidated and vulnerable sharing the road with them. The road begins to descend at an alarming rate, the gradient causing a dropping sensation. With 15% displayed on the road sign, we are given a clue as to why we are almost 'up the backside' of a bus, and why its brakes are burning acrid rubber.

The downward angle is so steep that I have a clear view directly over Nev's head. Bracing, by wedging myself between the triangle of the handlebars, seat and pedals, only just keeps me from sliding forward. Nev squeezes the brakes firmly but gently and a few seconds later releases them. He repeats this process to maintain a semblance of control, but each time he releases, I feel we are being catapulted and likely to face-plant into the rear of the bus.

"Don't worry," Nev reassures. "These brake discs are huge; they'll have no trouble holding us. I'm going to let them go for a bit now though, I can feel that they're getting hot."

I soften my elbows so they bend just a little, in an effort to relieve the tension, and feel I should force myself to rely on the stopping capacity of the disc-brakes, 203mm in diameter on the front and 180mm on the rear. My elbows quickly become rigid again as Nev continues "If they get too much hotter there will be friction burn and they'll be useless! I reckon they're having trouble holding all our weight on this gradient."

Sun filled Drumnadrochit is a welcome interlude; time to sit on a seat that is broader than fifteen centimetres, rest, eat ice-cream and take in the pretty scenery. This is the home of the Loch Ness Monster, and all of the 'Nessy' paraphernalia overwhelmingly dominates the souvenir shop. The little green monster is presented in a ludicrous variety of guises, predominantly as a harmless cute character; in the form of soft toys for babies, plastic pencil toppers for school children, and even decorative golf club covers for adults! An entire industry has been created around a monster, whose presumed sightings have been witnessed and recorded numerous times since the 6th Century. We are only twelve miles from the Youth Hostel so can afford the time to relax and loiter amongst the souvenirs and whiskey displays.

Our enjoyment of this sunny afternoon is extended as we take a walk out to the ruins of Urquhart Castle. The castle has been a pivotal point in the turbulent history of Scotland, having been through many conflicts, particularly during the 500 years from the early 1200's to the late 1700's. Built on a rocky outcrop and surrounded on three sides by water 600 feet deep; now the dilapidated structure, with open vantage, contributes to the romance of the Loch, and the possibility of sighting the elusive monster.

Our final ride of the afternoon is back on to the busy A82 that hugs the shore of Loch Ness. The stream of traffic has felt threatening and we are pleased to finally arrive at the Youth Hostel. There is peacefulness here, even though the buildings are adjacent to the busy main road. The serene water-filled view, draws the eye and the noisy threat of the constant traffic is soon forgotten, replaced by the lapping of water on the pebbly shore.

Sitting on the bottom bunk of our twin room, I am reflecting on the day. I think the books were wrong. I feel a great sense of accomplishment having survived day three, with body and emotion intact. The day has been long and quite difficult at times, but overall easily achievable. I have learned two things today. Nev really did know what he was doing when he ordered the Fandango. I have affectionately started referring to the tandem as the 'beast'. Our black beast is large, strong and awkwardly recalcitrant but together we are slowly dominating its spirit. Secondly, I need to encourage Nev to call 'granny' his friend!

Day Three Stats:

Distance covered: 105 kilometres, 66.52 miles

Maximum speed: 56.9 kph

Average speed: 20.3 kph

Steepest hill, descent 15%

Riding time: 5 hours 11 minutes

Trip Miles total: 175.95.

Loch Ness - Glencoe

Day Four: UK
Saturday, 9th June

The hostel is nestled, squashed between the main road and the Loch shoreline. Wisps of morning mist hug the shore and allude to a lurking monster.

The day starts with the routine that we have fallen into. Breakfast is accompanied by the relevant pages to the days intended route. We had torn only the pages mapping this journey from the 2007 Phillip's Road Atlas of Britain, and we now spread a few of them on the table. We also have our PDA - Personal Digital Assistant - that stores the Excel spreadsheet that is our 'electronic guide'. While in Australia we had ordered the very comprehensive CTC, End to End Guide, however these printed directions were for those travelling in the more popular direction of Lands End to John O'Groats (LEJOG). I had spent many hours reversing all of the directions and documenting them on an Excel spreadsheet, with a separate worksheet for each day. At the last minute we had decided that we should get more IT savvy and take a PDA with us that had wireless internet access. This would have the important weight reducing advantage of not carrying bulky heavy books and papers and as a bonus, would also give us access to our children using SKYPE and email. We did however have a back-up plan having also brought with us the printed pages from the original LEJOG guide, just in case all systems failed.

Today we have a fifty-five mile ride ahead of us. We linger over the directions. There is an alternative route, described in our guide as mostly off-road, but rideable on a 'touring cycle' that we could take into the forests, and then travel on forest roads alongside Loch Lochy. We seriously consider the option as riding on tarmac has never been our preferred riding surface. For us there is nothing more satisfying than riding in a forest and it appears that this route may only be a little demanding physically, with only a few minor aspects that may be technically challenging. Too challenging just brings the walker out in me! The peace of the forest is a tempting alternative, even for a short period away from the main road.

With our decision made, to battle the traffic rather than enjoy the peace of the forest, and with breakfast cleared, we pack the panniers. We each have one of the large fifty-four litre panniers for our individual items. All clothing is rolled and stuffed as deeply and as tightly as possible, so that other personal items can fit. Stowed in one of the small front panniers of twenty-eight litres is an assortment of shared items including stainless steel bowls, mugs, knives, forks and spoons. A small 'Billy' for cooking and a 'Pocket Rocket' gas stove complete the kitchen ware. A plethora of tools and 'spares' fill the other small pannier: derailleur hanger, tyre, two inner tubes, 'Sram' chain links, bike pump, two gear cables, five spokes, 'Allen' keys, chain breaker, 13mm ring, open-end spanner and a bike lock with 1.8 metres of 'bike lock cable'.

At 9.30 a.m. we are finally ready to depart. We can be added to the list of tourists leaving the loch without sighting 'Nessie'!

The mist has already dissipated to reveal a sun-filled morning. I'm feeling good about the journey to this point and we begin the day with a flat ride along the edge of the loch. We can see the alternative route we had debated, high above us, and congratulate ourselves on the decision to contend with the main road traffic rather than the challenging height of the Great Glen Way.

At Fort Augustus, built after the 1715 Jacobite uprising, we leave the loch and follow the Caledonian Canal, which was opened in 1822 and built to provide a short-cut for boats between the east and west coasts of Scotland. Alone, as we cycle along the tow path, it is very peaceful, adjacent to the River Oich. Surrounded by stunning scenery, the view from the canal path is of distant woods, nestled beneath dark hills. The flat terrain is a bonus for our legs this morning and leads us gently to re-join the main road through Invergarry to the shores of Loch Lochy.

Today is Saturday, and the sunshine attests to summer having finally arrived in Scotland. It seems as if every Scotsman is out for a weekend drive! Back on the main road the traffic is heavy. Vintage cars have also now joined the foray!

Peering over Nev's shoulder I see an on-coming car ease out and duck back in. It does this again and causes my senses to sharpen. I feel as if I can see the driver's split second thought process computing. *Anything coming? Yes. Wait a second. Check again. Anything coming? No. Okay be quick there isn't much time. Step hard on the gas. Pull wide.* I see the car suddenly swerve out into the right-side lane of the road. Suddenly we are faced with the car coming at us head on! The driver's surprise is etched on his face. He had pulled out wide on the narrow road, never expecting in his path, a tandem! A scream escapes me as Nev desperately hugs the verge in an effort to avoid being splattered on the tarmac. Momentarily, two frightened people astride a tandem are wondering if they are going to exist for longer than this moment! Split second thoughts of family and then... the fearful moment is past. The brief 'near-miss' encounter was way too close for comfort!

The Commando Memorial, and our Mini, in which we completed a tour in the UK in 1977

Legs that have become quivering and jelly-like, barely give enough momentum to force the tandem to continue the climb. At the Commando Memorial at the hill's crest, we welcome the opportunity to rest and settle our adrenalin pumped heart beats. The imposing memorial is dedication to those commandos who trained in the local area, and gave their lives during the Second World War. It's an avid reminder of the destruction of war. The bronze sculpted soldiers gaze toward Ben Nevis and the distant ranges, as if seeking strength from the boldness of the mountains.

Flat paddocks, where long haired black sheep chew the lush grass, draw our eyes towards the town of Fort William, a settlement that came into existence as a Fort; constructed to control the population, after Oliver Cromwell's invasion during the English Civil War. The fort was later used as a post to suppress the Jacobite uprisings of the 18th Century. In the distance Fort William nestles on the shores of Loch Linnhe, under the shadow of Ben Nevis, and the surrounding mountains. A well-deserved lunch-stop is scheduled, but first we stretch our legs, wandering down the High Street, a pedestrian-only precinct. Later lunch is washed down with a cold glass of lemonade, in the comfort of the Ben Nevis Hotel established in 1806. Our progress today has been pleasing, but we are still feeling nervous, following the near-miss and contending with the heavy traffic.

We stop to take a photo. Nev stays with the tandem while I snap the picture. Back on the bike I have taken my seat; and clipped both feet into the pedals. My departure preparations completed, I am, as usual, ready to pedantically follow the text-book tandem instructions that will ensure an easy take-off. Meanwhile, Nev has been 'holding' the tandem. He has been able to remain seated as, with a kerb on his left, he has additional height, allowing his left foot to be balanced on the kerb and his right foot remains clipped-in. This is not Nev's usual starting stance, but he indicates we are ready to go. I only have one job as 'stoker' and this I take very seriously. My only, but very important role, is to start the tandem! I attempt to do my usual few fast pedal rotations, to create movement and maintain balance, but for some reason Nev thwarts my efforts and 'hops' along the grass, on his left foot. We finally get moving in unison, but Nev is clearly in pain having twisted his knee!

"What on earth were you doing" I snap. "It's my job to start us off!"

"I was concerned that a full circle of the pedals would cause them to hit the kerb; we might have been tipped off."

We decide that in future we will always begin by following the exact science that has, up to this point, always been successful. I will be seated at the rear, feet 'clipped-in', while Nev will be in a standing position, straddling the frame, with each foot firmly planted on the ground. I will give Nev my usual verbal warning "turning," to give him some notice that I am about to rotate the pedals so he can take evasive action to avoid being 'clunked' in the back of his calf muscle by a pedal; a painful sensation that he has already experienced many times on this trip. I will rotate the pedals so that the left pedal is highest. Then, with Nev balanced, standing on his right foot, left foot 'clipped-in' on the high side, I will start pedalling, not too frantically, so that Nev can raise his backside to the seat while continuing to pedal with his left leg! Once motion is achieved, Nev will then clip his right foot into the pedal, as soon as his other leg catches up with the rotations.

In spite of our anxiety about sharing the road with heavy traffic, there is no alternative route. The distance covered has already taken us through two 'map pages' and we are moving onto the road network displayed on the third page of the day, as we continue on the main A82 alongside Loch Linnhe, the largest seawater loch in Scotland. The afternoon traffic is not as heavy, but we are now being passed intermittently by vehicles laden with cycles and kayaks.

Chatting easily to each other through our headsets, memorable activities of times past are recalled. When we lived in New Zealand, in the period of our lives from our early 30's to mid 40's, we both got a great deal of satisfaction from participating in, or helping set up and marshal at, multi-sport events. Often Nev would compete in a team with his more superior athletic male friends. I would also be participating as a team member with a group of my girlfriends.

Occasionally we entered events as a couple; with Nev taking on the kayak and cycle sections and I would fill the middle discipline, a twelve to twenty kilometre cross-country run! I feel the faint surge of an adrenaline rush just in sharing our recollections of these past activities. Those events were such an adventure. Pitting the body against the demands of the various sports; whether a long cycle section, a forest run or tackling the swift rivers; it was always the desire to succeed that drove the body. The success was to finish; never the expectation of winning, as that prospect was unattainable for us in the mixed-team category. Senses were always heightened while competing. Adrenaline kicks caused rushes to the system, for sometimes up to twenty-four hours beyond the event. The physical effort was only ever for a couple of hours, followed by relaxing and socialising with other contestants, yet each event always culminated in feelings of total exhaustion. Those exertions now seem small and quite insignificant when compared to this epic journey. We have chosen to undertake day after entire day of maximum effort. By the end of today we will have completed four days. One quarter of our journey.

Recollecting those earlier experiences, we somehow feel a connection with the activity happening here, as if the people in the vehicles that have been overtaking us could be those former contestants. Our efforts become more vigorous and we power towards Ballachulish, a small town from which we understand it is only three more miles to reach our destination, the Youth Hostel at Glencoe. The instructions to get to the hostel state that, from the A82 turn right at the Glencoe Hotel, and quickly right again towards Glencoe village; continue through the village along single track for two miles.

Continuing on the A82 and climbing steadily we notice, to our left, a cluster of tents, signifying a campground, and beyond that a clear highland river tumbles over pebbles. Pretty though it is, that vista isn't what we were expecting. We stop at the campground to ask for directions, as we have not come across the Glencoe Hotel yet. We are told that we have bypassed the village, and that the Youth Hostel is on the road behind the campground, and also beyond the river but there is no bridge across in our current vicinity. We are told that we should continue up the main road; eventually we will come across a minor road on our left that will lead to the Youth Hostel.

In spite of the small confidence boost that we felt earlier; for me this setback just highlights the weariness of my body which I have experienced even more towards the end of each afternoon. It wouldn't matter so much if the fatigue was confined to my muscles, but it seems to also become entrenched in my psyche, and my spirits slump. Our legs continue their weary climb up the steady gradient. If we were facing an incline such as this first thing in the morning, the effort would be negligible; however at this late time in the day I am tired, and annoyed that we had not been able to correctly decipher the directions! How could we have actually missed a town?

Continuing further up the broad valley, ahead of us the monolith of Bidean Nam Bian presents a stunning focal point, but my mind is stuck in annoyance mode! The road we seek eventually comes into view, and with a twist to the left, we have the pleasure of freewheeling downhill! The pleasure however is tempered by the thought that this means we will have to climb it first thing tomorrow. Our arrival time is 5.30 p.m. and the Youth Hostel is a welcome site. We have travelled an additional seven miles today, mostly climbing; that is a hefty punishment for a navigational error!

At the Youth Hostel we have our own room, and back there, after showering and dressing, we lie for fifteen minutes flat on our backs on the floor with our legs straight in the air and resting parallel against the wall. This position, we believe, may help drain the lactic acid from our weary leg muscles.

With villages now closer together, and having left the sparsely populated highlands behind, we are no longer worried about being stranded beside a road unable to continue due to lack of nourishment. Dinner tonight is our ration pack; a light-weight, freeze-dried, 'sachet' meal. Thirty years ago we had experienced camping in the UK, and it had been primitive back then. Ablution services were little more than long-drop toilets at the end of a farmer's mown paddock. We didn't trust that the UK may have moved into the 21st Century since then, with modern camping technology, so we brought the meal with us from Australia. Freeze-dried food has a reputation for being tasteless, but this one was a surprisingly delicious spiced chicken and cashew rice combination.

Saturday night, in the northern hemisphere with no responsibilities, sets Nev in the mood to party. We had noticed, as we freewheeled down towards the hostel, that we had passed Clachaig Inn. Early evening the hostel seems to empty, as people make their way in the direction of the Inn. Despite feeling weary, I too am keen to collect some memories, other than the soreness of my backside and strained legs! So we walk the short distance up to Clachaig Inn.

We have stumbled on a genuine piece of history and an evening that becomes one of the most memorable of the trip! Clachaig Inn is obviously a popular social venue on a Saturday, as we have to squeeze through the overflow of people standing in groups outside, on this balmy light-filled evening. Inside we spy a gentleman sitting alone at a table that is large enough for four. We slide onto the bench facing him as, at the same time, he is re-joined by his wife. There is a hint of annoyance from them at first, as their privacy is now broken. But we strike up a conversation. The couple are 'imports' from Lancaster, now living in this region, and they have come from marshalling at the multisport event today. It is easy for us all to chat having multisport marshalling in common. We share the packed 'Snug Bar' with a number of dogs, lying under their master's seats.

I am fascinated by the variety of vessels that hang above the bar; personal containers for the regulars to drink their 'daily' from. The huge selection of drinks on offer, line the wall behind the barman; shelves heavily stocked with at least 100 different varieties of whiskey! We sample a couple of the 'real' ales and pass a pleasant evening chatting, all the while being entertained by a Scottish Folk Band, playing their instruments; fife and bagpipe, 'fling out' notes that create an atmosphere of both gaiety and haunting.

This region is the home of the MacDonald Clan, and our evening of imbibing is held almost on the exact historic site of the attempt to eradicate them. Back in 1692 punishments were tough if you didn't obey the laws, and there was no such thing as freedom of speech or choice of allegiances. The new King, of both England and Scotland, was William 111. Four years previously he had deposed King James 11, a Scotsman. Various highland Clans had been rising up against William. King William offered the Highland clans a pardon for their misdemeanours, as long as they pledged their allegiance to him before 1 January 1692. Many clansmen did the sensible thing and duly complied. I don't think they were being disloyal but rather acted from self-preservation, to avoid death, which was the penalty if they did not obey.

Now a loyal man can't easily change his convictions and allegiances from one man to another, just because he is ordered to. Alasdair Maclain, 12th chief of Glencoe, of the clan MacDonald, was such a man. He waited for James 11 to give him permission to 'release his chief's oath' to him, before travelling to Fort William to deliver the demanded pledge to William. Although Maclain received the awaited release mid-December, he left his journey until the last possible day. Maclain, got to Fort William and was told he had to travel on to Inverary. The weather was bad – it was after all the middle of winter, and this is Scotland – and to add to his difficulties, Maclain got put in detention at Balcardine Castle. Later, when he finally got to Inverary, he found that Campbell, who had to receive his pledge, was away. Because of the delay in leaving something so important to the last minute, Maclain must have been a very worried man. However he eventually followed all the stipulated criteria and returned home satisfied that he had met the requirements.

On 12th February the MacDonalds had been offering their hospitality to two companies of soldiers under the command of Captain Robert Campbell. A Captain Drummond arrived with orders for Campbell to wipe out the MacDonald rebels with whom they were staying. Maclain was murdered as were thirty-eight other MacDonald clansmen, and forty women and children also died of exposure after their homes were burned. Somehow a few MacDonald clansmen escaped, and have passed on, even to this day, the message: 'never trust a Campbell'.

Day Four Stats:

Distance travelled: 101.53km, 64.82 miles

Maximum speed: 50.8 kph

Average speed: 22.6 kph.

Riding time: 4 hours 28 minutes

Total trip miles: 240.77

Glencoe - Loch Lomond

Day Five: UK
Sunday, 10th June

Our day starts with the climb we were expecting out to the A82. Again we have no choice of route as this is the only road that we will travel fifty-five miles, to our destination on Loch Lomond. This main thoroughfare has two lanes, one in each direction; a very narrow sealed verge is to be our space. Vehicles constantly pass, barely leaving space between metal panels and handlebars; a heady mix of motorcycles ducking into tight spaces, cars, vans and caravans as the Scots head to summer holiday destinations. The motorbikes are the worst. Their throaty rumbling comes from behind, ever so briefly tame at first, deepening into an ominous roar that threatens my heart to stop in frightened expectation of an attack from the rear. I am conscious of becoming tenser as each motorbike overtakes and Nev feels my nervousness as rigidity transferring through the bike frame. We stop briefly to regain confidence but it is quickly shattered when we resume riding again, as the racing traffic is constant.

Ahead we can see the gentle climb we will ascend as the road slices through this broad U-shaped valley that was formed by an ice-age glacier. Our climbing continues steadily until we conquer The Pass of Glencoe. The reward for our efforts is a bleak vista of large boulders and tussock, across Rannoch Moor, an area of some fifty square miles. A lone fisherman is silhouetted in the shore waters of a small Lochan, a tiny picture of human serenity dwarfed beside the wind shaken tussock and surrounding highlands. The morning progresses in steady achievement, conquering each hill and being thankful that we have not been taken-out by the horrendous traffic.

Lunch is well timed with our arrival at the small village of Lyndrum. The 'Perfect Spot' looks like a popular lunch venue. The cafe advertises 'real good, Scottish home cooking' and Cullen Skink, in spite of the name, is too tempting to bypass. This is a very delicious, thick broth, made from peat-smoked haddock, potatoes, and onion; cooked in milk and cream.

The barren highland passes are behind us now and we are making speedy progress. The scenery has changed to greener pastoral hues and the road appears to narrow, encroached upon by the shrubbery of lilac coloured azaleas growing alongside.

We feel the unexpected loft in our raincoats as they unfurl and flap. The tandem is tossed like a little yacht with a freight ship bearing upon it.

"Whoa!" I yell as Nev grabs at the handlebars with the intensity of a captain at the tiller. The tempest created by an overtaking fully-loaded logging truck, leaves us shaken. We ease off, rotating the pedals slowly while consoling each other, thankful to have survived. Almost immediately another logging truck passes. Fortunately the second driver must have noticed the earlier turbulence and gives us a wider berth. The ensuing vehicular created vortex, though not so turbulent, still leaves us dazed and feeling rather vulnerable.

The weather is turning into a dismal drizzle, but the adrenaline rush that kicked in from the preservation instinct, gives enough of a high to negate any feelings of despondency because of the moisture.

In spite of the damp we decide to stop for ice-cream on the shores of Loch Lomond. While enjoying our treat we are entertained, at a distance, by a young piper who is playing for a group of tourists as they board a boat. His tartan hat, up-turned, is filling fast as coins are tossed in acknowledgement of his raucous talent.

Carrying more than one novel each between us, yet no tourist information so that our weight will be light, I haven't decided if we are foolish or empowered because we know nothing. Travelling with only loose map pages and the directions of the CTC guide, we are blissfully unaware of missed opportunities. Our lack of tourist information is intentional, as a site worth visiting at even as little as three miles away from our intended route, would usually equate to six return miles. Too far, when added to a day that is already set at a distance we will only just be able to accomplish. Every delightful spot that comes unexpectedly into view is therefore a treasure, and this is how we feel on our discovery of the village of Luss. Our decision to stop for a drink is based on the village's proximity to today's final destination. With only fifteen miles left to cycle, and as it is only five o'clock, we have time for lemonade at the local Colquhoun Arms Hotel. Despite it not yet being night-time the hotel is full of couples and families enjoying their evening meal. The food smells delicious but this is a brief afternoon tea interlude for us. Refreshed, we cross to the main road and wander the prettiest village we have seen to date. Streets are lined with identical, slate roofed, square cottages built in stone, with gardens neatly tended.

Back on the tandem, with fifteen miles to travel, we at last have the pleasure of riding on a cycle lane beside the lake and peacefully buffered from the traffic noise by thick shrubbery. The drizzle has recommenced on our leaving Luss. Always a fine weather person I am determined to focus on the beautiful scenery, rather than the deteriorating weather, as we ride parallel with the foreshore, and I decide to block out the rain by absorbing the pretty misted view of the Loch that is Lomond. Thoughts of high road and low road spring to mind and the verse of the song, learned in childhood, spins out of control in my head. Drizzle has a tendency to become more persistent precipitation and on this occasion does as expected. For the first time on this trip, we stop to don leggings, so are now protected in full wet-weather gear.

"Almost there" Nev says "and tonight we have a drying room and meals available so we'll buy dinner".

We know that the stately home is to the right of the road. Riding on a cycle path behind bushes, and on the left side of the road concerns me. We are soon riding easily on account of a very slight downward gradient, following parallel along the fence line of grand properties. The signs tell us we are on the outskirts of Balloch. We ask for directions and my fears become reality. The Youth Hostel is now two miles away, but behind us.

A slight elevation returns us back along the footpath to the hostel entrance we had missed on the other side of the busy highway. It is not so easy to negotiate the steep gravel driveway. Tired pedal strokes force the cycle tyres to track through the stones that roll like marbles. The driveway cuts through the park-like expanse of lawn, delivering us to a very impressive stately home that is to be our accommodation for the night. The grand exterior of fawn coloured stone exudes warmth while the ornate portico is a welcoming feature. From the house there are stunning views of Loch Lomond and Ben Lomond (974m) beyond.

On checking our reservation the desk clerk tells us we have booked dormitories. Oh no not again! We are quite sure this is not the case. Fortunately there is an unoccupied dormitory that we can have all to ourselves. The next unsuspecting blow is delivered.

"I'm sorry but the restaurant is closed tonight. The chef has returned to his family to deal with a crisis and no meals are available."

As has become habitual at the end of each day, the route to our room – this time a loft room on the fourth floor - involves lugging the bags up flights of stairs. The end of day ritual then begins. I find the easiest way to access my gear is to pull everything out of the panniers and spread the contents all over the room. The set of fresh clothes is then more easily located. A trip to the bathroom usually involves washing of the body as well as there is always the day's cycle clothing to be washed. Usually I trample my dirty clothes on the floor of the shower before rinsing, but tonight we have access to a laundry and washing machines. On the many occasions when there isn't a drying room, the hand wrung clothing is hung to drip-dry, slung over backs of chairs, bunk railings or anywhere in the room that will be advantageous to the overnight drying process.

The impressive stately home that is the Loch Lomond Youth Hostel

Showers are such reviving water features and just as well because if we want to eat tonight we have no choice but to ride back down into Balloch.

A local pub presents an interesting menu. We pass on the haggis meal and instead choose revitalizing pasta.

Fortunately this far north, even though it is 9.30 p.m. the daylight lingers long enough for us to ride the two miles back to the hostel without needing the assistance of lighting. To complete the exercise program for the day we drag our weary bodies up the flights of stairs for the fifth time.

At last we can relax and make the most of a good night's sleep that is so important for recovery, as tomorrow we do it all again. "Nev I'm so excited about getting closer to our day off. I reckon having got this far I will be okay to make it for another three days; I reckon I'm getting stronger," I murmur just before sleep overtakes me.

A disembodied voice wafts towards my ear. Is it the ghost that is supposed to live here?

"Sorry Lou, you've miscalculated. It's actually four days of riding until we reach Chester."

Not the ghost, just Nev with the dispiriting news. That is only one more day than I had anticipated, but I now wonder if it is going to be achievable or a nightmare.

Day Five Stats:

Distance travelled: 98.65 kilometres, 61.30 miles

Total trip miles: 301.77

Loch Lomond - Wanlockhead

Day Six: UK
Monday, 11th June

Making good use of the facilities has resulted in clothes that are clean and dry, camera and PDA batteries charged, and in the large dormitory space we have spread out all our items and done a stock-take. We had set off from home carrying what we thought was the minimum of everything, yet there are now clearly some possessions we can do without. I had the misconception that while cycling though the UK we might take in an evening movie or other outing for which I would want to be clothed just a little bit more femininely than in lycra or over- shorts. For such an eventuality I was carrying a lightweight summer dress and strappy sandals but they were more specifically to be worn to dinner at the Eiffel Tower in Paris later in this trip. Clearly this outfit was not going to be necessary at this point in our travel. Nev is convinced he can do without his jacket, and these items are bundled together with a couple of novels, parcelled and posted to friends in Surrey. We will catch up with our package at the end of this ride.

With our load lightened by four kilograms we expect to make good progress over the sixty-five miles we will cover today; however the weight still straddling the frame of the bike means the reduction is not noticeable at all. We do however feel light-hearted, as the ride starts today with the luxury of travelling for some distance, along a flat cycle path beside a canal. The breathlessly still air reflects upside down cottages in the calm canal waters.

Obstacles in the form of wooden rails threaten to upset the calm. The barriers are wisely installed to keep cyclists' speed down. I have always enjoyed the technical challenge while riding on my own bicycle, of trying to twist to the right, and then u-bend to the left, without touching the railings. The constant interruptions though are quite unwelcome on this trip, as the tandem is too long to negotiate narrow turns. Nev becomes frustrated with the interruptions. I can only sympathize as at each barrier there is no option but to lift the beast over. Fortunately the wooden rails are low, so Nev manhandles the fully laden bike himself. The quick heave and hoist action, is better than having to bother wasting the time involved in removing and then refitting the panniers. Nev's uttering of expletives becomes more colourful but gives the boost of strength required.

The cycle path leads us the eighteen miles into Glasgow along an embankment that used to support a railway line. Three men sitting on camp chairs beside the path and drinking beer, make an unusual welcoming committee as it is only mid-morning and we are seemingly in the middle of nowhere. Trying not to draw attention to ourselves we slip by silently but the "Hey, she's not pedalling!" catches the breeze and blows towards my ear. The jibe, just another of the many we have already heard, always implying lack of effort on my part, follows us down the track and deeper into the city of Glasgow.

My foreman at the Heinz Factory in London was George, and I am reminded of the little Glaswegian whose thick Scottish brogue was a foreign language to me. I would try to tune into his accent but, with the noise of the cans as they rattled across the overhead conveyors, it was impossible to hear speech, let alone understand. Even though it was mandatory to wear ear muffs that muffled the cacophony, I would usually have to watch the direction George waived his hands and try to decipher what was to be done.

I was employed in quality control. The first role I had was to work from a little office room, adjacent to the main factory floor with two other staff. Every thirty minutes, one woman collected ten cans from the production line that contained only steam-swollen beans. The other woman would move to the same machine but to an area that was at a more advanced stage in the production process, to collect ten cans containing beans with sauce. These cans and contents were weighed and the weights recorded. The objective was to ensure that the quantity of beans did not exceed the optimum, or the final sealed product may be too dry or too liquid. My part in this team was to relieve these two staff while they had their tea breaks and lunch break, and weekly manicure. For the remaining five hours each day, I sat in the locker room reading novels. There was a time too, when we, along with another group of staff from a different department, had the surprising task of tipping out the steam-cooked beans from a selection of cans and counting them. I found this an extremely tedious job that became worse when we had to swap cans with the person next to us, and had to recount the beans from their can. If our tally didn't match we had to start again.

There is no way we can avoid contact with the city of Glasgow as our route has foretold our course. We are instructed to *'follow cycleway from Loch Lomond-Glasgow. This uses canal paths and disused railway lines (some rubbish). Take footbridge over dual carriageway - past several car parks, Conference Centre & Scottish Exhibition. Turn Right Cross River Clyde on Victoria Bridge, continue down Gorbals St, under railway bridge, going diagonally Right to crossroads with Pollokshaws Rd. Left over railway bridge. Cathcart Rd. Cont Straight Over at junction with B763, Aikenhead Rd (A728) turn Left past playing fields & school (Prospecthill Rd). At next crossroads Straight Over across A730. Go Straight Over A749. Continue to Rutherglen(B768).* And that is just what we do.

The ride through Glasgow is mostly on cycle ways, and in spite of the comprehensive directions, we keep losing sight of the route. This necessitates stopping repeatedly to consult the instructions. Nev is frustrated with our failure to comprehend the directions and displays his annoyance by dropping down roadside kerbs so we are travelling in traffic. He is insisting that it is dangerous to follow footpath-like cycle routes, because every time we come to a side road, we have to be doubly wary, checking that approaching traffic does not barge through and cut us off. So, as Nev is the captain, I must follow. We are out in the traffic, which I find alarming, particularly when it comes to negotiating roundabouts. Nev's approach to these is to situate us smack in the middle of the left-hand lane. He reckons that we are safer holding our place on the road, with the same rights as a vehicle. His theory is that the drivers will clearly see us and have to sit behind, or give us a wide berth. Less likely to be knocked off, he reckons, however I do not feel any less intimidated taking this approach.

Glasgow is by-passed. Well not really. We are riding directly through the city, yet the only tourist view we have is of the exteriors of buildings. I need to be more demanding as my utterance of "Oh look there Nev, we're just passing the Art Gallery," is taken purely as the statement it is, and I find myself peeping through the rails of the bridge to admire the river scene as we cross and continue on our way. We haven't needed to confirm directions with anyone so do not even have the opportunity to hear that wonderful Glaswegian accent.

The road leaving Glasgow leads into gentle climbing. With the temperature around twenty-five degrees Celsius this is our warmest day. The sun is actually burning my skin, a sensation I didn't expect to have in the UK.

I have never experienced a British summer, having arrived many years ago at the beginning of winter, and then leaving back in 1976 for Europe in the first week of June. Although June is the official beginning of the English summer, in that year we hadn't been given any hint of the warmth that was to come after we left the island. We found it amusing, as we sunned ourselves in the forty degrees of the Mediterranean, that the news from England reported that they were experiencing a heat wave. Day after day of temperatures similar to what we are experiencing today, had caused people to die and created such a thirst, that quenching it had resulted in the pubs running out of beer.

Glasgow suburbs climb sedately towards the countryside. The pace is steady; the climbing is a gentle enough gradient, to notice only a little extra effort is being required. The sun's warmth tingles on my arms and the city tension is soothed by the music we are playing over the intercom.

Green countryside stretches before us, with long flat bitumen mapping the route ahead. Way off in the distance, a range of shaded hills is darkly ominous, but I anticipate we will go via a valley to our destination.

On the outskirts of Hamilton we come across our first British Supermarket. It strikes me as surprising that we have not encountered any other 'real' supermarket until this point in our travels. I realise then, that our cycle guide has been taking us to the outer edge of a town or village and then directing us toward the next without us actually going near real suburbia.

Generally I hate supermarket shopping as it is usually a duty jammed into a day already full of other chores. On this occasion it is with wonder that I stroll along the aisles, astounded at how much prepared food is displayed. Now I pride myself on being a good cook. In fact I have this personal philosophy, that is probably quite warped for this day and age, whereby I generally refuse to cook with the aid of sachets and jars. By that, I mean I cook in the manner of recipe and fresh ingredients. I was awestruck by the vegetables already peeled, grated or sliced; presented in air-tight plastic packets, to maintain freshness. Signage on paper packages indicate various other contents within these packs, a selection of boxes and sachets; containers of everything needed for a Chinese, Mexican or other delectable meal. All products are graphically displayed on the box enticing the busy browser to purchase the entire contents to create a gourmet delight. I wonder if the art of cooking has been forgotten in this country. As we leave the supermarket the true answer comes to light. Immediately in front of the supermarket the tarmac signage indicates parking for the disabled, covering an area the size of a football field; I counted space for 100 cars. This is quite funny considering there isn't a single car in any of the vacant spaces. Maybe a huge proportion of the population is disabled and can't dice and slice their vegetables and they only visit the supermarket on weekends.

At a great height, and a long way in the distance, I notice a white bulbous blob that looks like it may be a tower or similar. I stare at it and then dismiss an anxious thought. Surely we couldn't possibly be going anywhere near that lofty landmark?

From Glasgow the incline has been steady all afternoon. Having arrived at Crawfordjohn, our turn off, and gazing at the vista spread out below us I reckon that this surely must be the highest point of our ride today. We are literally perched atop a T-intersection. Stopping briefly to check the guide notes; I glance to our left and sure enough, the narrow road is the one that we must take. This descent can be described as a decline, both because with a rougher looking surface and width narrowing to lane, it is a sudden deterioration of the route to this point; and also because it is a plunge rather than a slope. We can see where the road levels out at a stream, at least a five hundred meter drop, virtually straight-down, and then our route disappears around a corner behind pine trees; flat from here on, I hope.

Down we plummet at stomach dropping speed; I restrain myself from letting out a blood curdling scream (in fun rather than fear) and press against the handlebars so I'm not thrust into Nev's back.

The pretty stone bridge takes us across the river and past a gypsy camp hugging the riverside. We glide past their little encampment, round the corner and lose the warmth from the sun.

The light dissipates into shadow as we commence climbing steeply and then ever so much more steeply again. The effort of the ride today suddenly catches up with me and I am feeling exhausted, but we are approaching another bend and surely the road will be level around the corner? Disappointment sets in as we have no choice but to climb a little more, negotiate the bend and face yet another hill; up again. *'Come on girl, suck it in, you're almost there, keep it going'* becomes my mantra.

Whenever I have to seriously apply myself to overcome physical exertion, I take big suck-it-in breaths attempting to draw as much oxygen as possible into my lungs. Nev finds my approach to deep oxygen-sucking breaths rather odd. In contrast, I find his short, sharp, little intakes of breath unusual. That we begin discussing the quirkiness of each other's method of breathing, and not for the first time on this trip, should really just be an indicator that we are both tired. Instead of just accepting that breathing is something that we do differently for whatever physiological reason; we each express our quite different point of view, and defend our own position. No matter what the method of oxygen intake, the benefits from this energy source do nothing to relieve the exertion that I am extending to climb a little more, negotiate another bend and climb a little more.

Our guide notes are directing us to Wanlockhead, referred to as the highest village in Scotland. My brain cells must be really fried, as I wonder why it has never registered with me, before this moment, that in order to achieve that status, the village must in reality be lofty. For us to get within reach of Wanlockhead must necessitate a significant amount of climbing effort. This delayed realisation has come to fruition. I can't focus on anything else except for the exhaustion that I am desperately trying to conquer.

I have completely lost interest in this epic. What a fool thing to even attempt. What the hell are we doing this for? "Who was the idiot who suggested this?" I yell into Nev's back.

I curse that article I saw in the Escape section of the Sunday Mail newspaper and my foolishness at even drawing 'Seven holidays for the Adventurer' to Nev's attention. I had joked that we could cycle the length of Britain, and maybe we should; while our legs still turned around. I posted the clipping to the notice board without another thought. Little did I know that Nev would run with the idea? I began to feel just a little concerned when weeks later, quite unexpectedly, Nev commented that he had been researching the trip and we should go to the UK next year.

So here I was again, in our life as a couple, participating in a situation that had the potential to be life changing and that I didn't really feel entirely comfortable with. How could Nev have known what I truly felt? After all I had initiated the thought process and had gone along with it; not saying much, all because I had been either too reticent to let my true feelings show, or didn't have the guts to indicate that I was actually thinking *'No, not a great idea for me'*. Eight years ago I had gone along with a significant idea that Nev had; to apply for work in another country. I had been somewhat unsure about such a major upheaval to our lives, but failed to voice my doubts. Before I knew it, I was transported from New Zealand to Australia, to set up a new life for myself and my family. This time, I am turning my exhausted legs around and around, feeling wretched and thoroughly pissed off!

The main street of the village of Leadhills is still inclining.

"I've had enough! I have to stop."

Much as I loathe giving in, my negativity has taken control of my will. Nev pulls over to let me walk. The change of working muscles is somewhat relieving. Nev is beside me pushing the tandem but I can't stay with the determination of his stride. I grip my hand under the back seat intending to offer my assistance, but this is quickly negated by Nev's speed. Instead of contributing to the push, I feel like I am being dragged along or worse still, may be holding back Nev's effort to maintain pace and forward momentum.

Nev insists on riding on his own and makes better progress turning his strong legs, rather than having to push this cumbersome recalcitrant beast. I am jogging the incline of the main street of Leadhills, and still cannot keep up.

Leadhills is a village founded on lead mining that operated from the 1100's, and was joined by mining of gold from about 1500. Although mining ceased in 1928 the village has survived through the resurrection of a tourist railway attraction that runs from Leadhills to Wanlockhead. If the train was running at this time I would have taken it. Right now though, I have no choice but to remount and contribute rotational leg effort to get us through a few more miles of countryside.

At last we reach the road apex and then begin to descend. The signpost, signifying our arrival at the village, claims that Wanlockhead is in fact at 1531 ft (467 m), the highest village in Scotland.

One of the few occasions when the ride got too much. Pushing through Leadhills.

Lotus Lodge Independent Hostel is in front of us and we have to apply just one more effort to negotiate through the gate and up a little pinch-climb that is the short driveway. The panniers are unclipped and we follow the directions to our room, lugging our gear up the stairs to the top floor. The 7.50 p.m. arrival time notes this day as the longest so far and my exhaustion is intense. I glance out the window across the village shrouded in evening mist, and spy to my horror, on a distant but parallel hilltop, the tower that had been my early afternoon focal point.

This is a well presented private hostel, with little niceties such as soap supplied and we appreciate the fresh clean surroundings. We have cooked and cleared away our dinner things and are now sitting opposite each other deep in our own thoughts. I try to take my mind off my weariness. I have got this far by taking one hour at a time, and then another until the first day was completed. Then I assured myself if I could cope with one day, I would have the confidence and ability to get through another. I have got through six days. The countdown is on now, as there are only three more cycling days until we can have an entire day out of the saddle.

Nev is sitting on the other opposite bottom bunk. He is also quietly reflective. Looking across he says, "This is the hardest thing I have ever done, and I can't believe that you are doing it with me!"

Day Six Stats:

Distance covered: 114.34 kilometres, 71.04 miles

Maximum speed: 53.7 kph.

The average speed of 17.9 km per hour is well below our usual average

Riding time: 6 hours 21 minutes

I have not recorded today's trip mileage total; clearly I have lost interest

Wanlockhead - Carlisle

Day Seven: UK
Tuesday, 12th June

W aking comes with physical weariness; a reminder of yesterday's epic. A young man at the hostel empathises with our exhaustion. While he had travelled from a southern direction, he was a number of days deeper into his journey and also feeling weary. His recommendation is, rather than to follow the route that would take us south-west through Mennock, and then from Thornhill to Dumfries down the A76, - described as *'what traffic there is on this road goes fast'* -that we should take an optional route using the National Cycle Network 74 that runs parallel with the A74 motorway. He had come that way yesterday and while it had been a steady climb for him, for us he reckoned it shouldn't be too physically demanding. The route, approximately sixty-two miles, will take us almost all the way to Carlisle and he told us it would probably be an enjoyable ride.

The two sets of brain cells we have between us have to tussle with the notion that initially we will be going in the wrong direction, adding some miles to the day's ride. Doubling back the short distance to Leadhills will be heading slightly north-east, not the south-easterly direction required to bring us directly towards our destination for the day. In the end logic prevails, and we set off back-tracking towards Leadhills, and then following the magically named Elvan Water to the village of Elvanfoot. I expect that as we had yesterday climbed to the highest village in Scotland, then from this point on, our journey will have to be downhill. Downhill all the way to Cornwall will be pivotal to ensuring the success of this trip I reckon.

The cycleway is actually a designated lane of the old B7078 dual-carriageway. Having been replaced by the M74 the B road is now an almost unused route and rather peaceful apart from the sound of thrumming vehicle tyres, wafting across from the distant motorway. Riding steadily down is the pleasure I desire, although these are interrupted by the occasional short climb, just to remind us not to be too complacent.

I keep glancing at the Speedo. "Nev I reckon my Speedo's broken down. It's stuck." I keep watching and then, after an age the number clicks over. "Oh no it's okay."

I keep watching, asking myself, *'why doesn't it change?'* I look around at the scenery, note the green rolling fields occasionally dotted with cows, then glance back to the computer. There is still no change. I'm just about to say something again and the number increases by one. I'm obsessed with catching the Speedo out. I stare at the motionless digits and just when I am convinced it really must be faulty, another mile is recorded.

"I hate miles," I moan into the intercom, "they are just slow and tedious; the speedo isn't broken." I don't want to be fixated on such a trivial little piece of technology, but I am repeatedly drawn to the monotony of waiting and watching; hoping that the mile will click over faster than the distance being recorded.

With our day off still three days ride away, we take this one as casually as we can. Moving in the required direction but interrupting the journey with occasional rests. Nev has promoted me to Captain for however long I want the helm. With the computer that is fixed to the front handlebar in view, I have the pleasure of watching the kilometres click by so much more quickly. The riding position is more upright and the different open perspective, uninterrupted, instead of blocked by back and helmet, is a welcome change.

On the back I have never really got comfortable with the riding position and have imagined that Nev, up front, was probably better off than me. Sitting on the back in the stoker role, the back handle bars to which I cling are fixed and rigid. Sure I have the advantage of letting my hands go if I want to, but generally I am gripping firmly. I could unclip my feet too and hold them outstretched, but rarely do. My body is supported by my backside that is always planted firmly on the seat. This is also the case for Nev. Unlike riding on a single mountain bike where the body weight is constantly shifting and raised off the seat, on the tandem there are few opportunities to stand on the pedals, taking the weight off the seat a little to relieve the pressure.

Even though I now have the front seat I am not feeling entirely comfortable with this experience either. Nev is wriggling and squirming. He comments, "We don't seem to be exactly upright. When I look down the centre of the top-tube it isn't perfectly in line with the bottom one."

He wants me to shift my weight on the seat to correct this, but when I adjust to give the bike an alignment that satisfies his pedantic demands, I feel like I am physically leaning to the right and slightly off balance. "You have got to be kidding! Can't you just relax back there?" I snap in response to his frequent suggestions for me to alter my seated position.

We are climbing a hill that to me, in the superior captaining position doesn't seem to be at all difficult. My legs are rotating easily with little resistance, so I don't believe I am hearing Nev's request. "Give me another gear, Lou."

How can that be? Clearly there is a noticeable difference in the amount of effort required when pedalling from the back. I knew it! All along I have been begging for more gears, obviously working harder than my Captain, and I have unnecessarily, been feeling a little inadequate.

Empowering though it is, to be away from traffic on a designated cycle lane, and to be in a position of control, I decide that I really don't want the responsibility of keeping us both upright and mobile. I have held the leadership position for only an hour. While it's been great to add steering and gear changing to the otherwise tedious role of leg turning, it hasn't taken long before the upright position has created a different pressure on my seat bones that I hadn't felt while stoking. Nev is still wiggling and fidgeting in an effort to have the bars parallel and I am getting pins and needles in my left hand, probably from gripping too tightly. There is also tightness in my jaw from clenching my teeth; which I reckon is directly attributed to trying not to rebuke the back seat carry-on.

Reluctantly I concede that the tandem, while heavy and fully loaded, is difficult for me to manage from the front seat. We have tried to keep the weight as low as possible. Having disposed of superfluous items days ago, we are down to a bike that weighs 30kg, carrying gear of 35kg, a Captain weighing in at 65kg and the Stoker at near 60kg; in all, a total weight of 190kg.

Navigating the direct route into a city is always easy; after all that is the direction that all signs point towards. We have been travelling with the motorway often in sight, but now we divert into little rural lanes. Peak hour, five o'clock traffic leaving Carlisle, is keenly headed towards us and homeward. The congested narrow road is intimidating. I consciously force myself to relax and even so, Nev comments that my lack of confidence is transferring through the frame, causing the bike to be more difficult to manoeuvre. Quite likely, I think, the same sensation I had felt in the morning during the period when he was Stoker!

The heavens open and heavy rain necessitates a quick stop, and rush to grab the raincoats. What a shame when we are so close to our destination.

The Cambro House Bed & Breakfast is on Warwick Street route A69. Our travel notes take us directly along this road so we will be well positioned for leaving Carlisle tomorrow. We pull off the access lane into the rear yard of the bed & breakfast. Although our coats have now dried in the early evening air, the clouds are still heavy with moisture and it is difficult to share the optimism of our host Dave, who is quite sure we will get our washing dry in spite of the conditions.

Rain is spitting on us as we walk the mile to the supermarket. Nev is salivating at the thought of roast chicken for dinner tonight. Disappointment sets in, however, when we make our way past the deli section only to find that department closed at 6 p.m. We appease our frustration by purchasing items that we intend to provide us with a picnic that we will lay out on the floor of our room: bread, coleslaw, and cold meats for a savoury feast followed by a dessert treat – a large sponge custard trifle that we will have to devour completely, as we do not have a refrigerator in the room to store it in. We can hear the rain pummelling the supermarket roof so delay leaving until the sound eases. The deluge has flooded the street guttering, and water is overflowing across the footpath. Negotiating our way back to the B&B becomes a game of hop-scotch as we leap puddles and hug the fence-lines. It is impossible to stay dry and we both roar with laughter as cars speeding through the road puddles, create air waves, showering us in sheets of water, an experience I have only ever witnessed while viewing a TV comedy program.

Day Seven Stats:

Distance covered 97.2 kilometres, 60.4 miles

Trip Miles total 433.21

Wow! We are in distance and days, halfway.

Carlisle - Kirkby Lonsdale

Day Eight: UK
Wednesday, 13th June

I comment on the beautiful contemporary kitchen at the B&B, as it is obviously quite new. Alice explains that back in January 2005, the equivalent of one month worth of rain fell in twenty-four hours, and gale force winds of sixty miles per hour battered this region. The River, only a few hundred meters along Warwick Road had overflowed, and the ground floor of this terrace house had been underwater to a depth of four feet.

I later discovered that the Bishop of Carlisle had expressed his sympathy, as you would expect from someone in an ecclesiastical position, for those who had been hit by that weather. However he went on to add that the problem with "environmental judgment is that it is indiscriminate." He reckoned that the introduction of pro-gay legislation had provoked God to act by sending the storms!

We start the day with a full English breakfast. I will need all the fortification I can get today. We are faced with an epic eighty miles and our guide notes warn we are in for a day that is difficult both navigationally, as well as for the distance to be covered. The notes recommend an interim hostel should be considered by those not certain about reaching the hostel at Slaidburn. With the number of days we have on leave from work, we have no choice but to make sure we conquer the full distance.

In the planning stage, while in the comfort of home, Nev had, because of his absolute confidence in our ability to complete this journey, dissuaded any fears raised by me. He had assured me that we would easily cover in a morning, the fifty to sixty mile distance usually set for each day. If I needed more than the one day of rest that we had allocated, then now and again we could have almost a twenty-four hour break. This would be achieved over a two day period. We would get to our destination early one day, because by Nev's reckoning we would easily complete a day's distance before lunch, and that would give us the afternoon for a break. Then the following day we could leave late – just before lunch - having the morning for rest. Nev expected we would easily complete that second day's allocated distance, in the afternoon.

"It will be summer after all and the daylight hours will be long," he'd said.

The reality to date is that we have each day, taken all of the entire day to cycle, and that has been with only minimal rest breaks.

Already today feels like it will be another of conquering, rather than enjoying, the distance we have set. Raincoats are donned and in spite of the current drizzle, our hope is that the depravity of the human race will not weigh too heavily on God's mind as we cover the next eighty miles.

Dave has given us directions that will ensure we easily get to the outskirts of town, so we expect to have a good start leaving Carlisle by the most direct route. The soft rain rolls into little balls on our Gore-Tex coats.

Today is going to be navigationally complex, a bit worrying because with the rain, it will be impractical to keep pulling the paper map and guide out for consultation. The guide notes have been studied but are too complex to commit to memory, as they are a plethora of directions that attest to much twisting and turning, to ensure that we remain on minor roads. While the guide is only in text, I imagine we are about to join the dots. As players in this childhood game, we will tandem from one village dot to the next with the lanes being our pencil line.

For the first nine miles we travel on narrow lanes. These climb to the top of each little hillock and down the other side. We are able to proceed quickly but cautiously. The village names on the signposts are not on our map and the villages on our map and guide are not displayed on the signposts. The signposts are not easy to find as the vigorous tendrils springing from the lush hedgerows have often enveloped the directions.

"What way is that one actually pointing?" I seek confirmation from Nev.

The post is slightly twisted and two very unclear choices point out from the tangle of hedge plants. We have turned numerous times right then left and have lost track of what road we are actually on. We figure we are quite near the B6263 – a road that we expected to only be travelling on for a mere 500 yards - and decide to continue on this route, until we have clear signage. Suddenly and unexpectedly, at a T-intersection we are facing the A6. This means we have already made a navigational error. The A6 appears on the map as a major road in the region so we are a little reluctant to take this route. In reality it is a dual carriageway that appears to be little used. We decide to forget about trying to navigate the scenic route and continue to travel the A6 for fifteen miles to Penrith. The map shows that just beyond Penrith we can rejoin our intended route.

We stop briefly in Penrith to buy sweets. I found, back at the beginning of our tour that my mouth kept feeling raspy and dry, especially in the mornings. This is possibly due to the overload on the one salivary gland that I have (I won't even contemplate the thought that it could be from my big, suck-it-in breathing style). The other gland had been removed when I was in my early 20's, as it had become strangulated by a neurofibromatosis. While sipping water was the best solution to overcoming the lack of moisture to the mouth problem, sipping resulted in excessive piddling, a condition I was attempting to avoid. In Scotland, on the third day into this journey I had brought the most delicious ginger toffee sweets. Testament to our self control, – not however for me in the bladder department, – we are now up to day eight and have only just depleted that first lolly bag supply. Alas the ginger toffees must have been a Scottish invention and the moisture to the mouth will now be administered to, by a toffee of less delectable prescription.

Two pedal strokes and our rotations are stopped abruptly. The chain has jammed. Nev removes the chain and discovers that two links have kinked. I silently suspect it may be because, having seated myself ready to start, I unintentionally rotated the pedals backwards, with quite a bit of my weight on them. Nev deftly breaks the chain, straightens the links, rejoins them and reattaches the chain. A two minute repair and we are on our way again.

Rain is now descending upon us with much more conviction. The news last night showed flooding in Northern Ireland (only 2cms from here on the map) as 55ml of rain had fallen there. The television screen portrayed Ireland hidden under a black band forecasting continuing rain. That ridge of low pressure is moving this way. My cycle computer drowns at 480.30 miles. I am disappointed as I cannot record the total trip mileage, but in truth I don't 'give a toss'. I no longer have to be frustrated by the mind-numbing, slow, mileage record. With my watch up my sleeve carefully protected from the rain; I can now be ignorantly oblivious to both distance and time.

We are having such a pleasant and surprisingly quiet ride on the A6 that we decide to continue to travel this route for a little longer. If the scenery is amazing on the other route that we had intended to be on, then it is too bad. We will never know what we have missed. We do know though, that we will not miss narrow lanes with their pinch climbs and bad signage that has already been experienced too often today.

Pretty as lanes are, we have come to realise that over the centuries advancements have been made in road engineering. This becomes obvious as soon as we leave the comfort of the A6 and turn left onto a lane towards Crosby Ravensworth. We can see the M6 motorway in the distance slicing broadly and gently on a minor gradient, carving easily through the forested valley. High above, hugging the valley wall, the older A6 we have so recently travelled, begins climbing steeply, cutting into the edge of the hill. We can see these two roads from this ancient lane that we have turned on to. We are high above the left side of a river that has cut so deeply into the earth that we cannot see into its watery depths. This lane, cool and dripping with moisture, is leading us into climbing steeply up and over a knoll, dropping sharply, climbing over another knoll, and continuing in this manner of graduated climbing, rather than following the contours. One of the descents is signed to warn of the 10% downward gradient. I am sure we have climbed many steeper gradients than that this afternoon. With wearying monotony, gaining more height each climb we finally summit; both feeling exhausted.

Nev decided he couldn't be bothered shaving every day.

Travelling along lanes blinkered by stone walls, or with hedgerows at least six feet high, on a tandem loaded with gear that is transporting us, who want to live longer than this adventure, we proceed with caution. Rather than the downhills being screamingly awesome, a frustrating too many of them run into blind corners that must be negotiated carefully, both to coax the tandem around the tightness of the bend and because we cannot be sure that we are not going to meet oncoming traffic. We cannot take advantage of any of the fast downward momentum that would usually thrust us partly up the ensuing steep climb.

The rain continues to be an annoying distraction. I find it hard to focus on anything other than the fact that the cool moisture is hampering my enjoyment. Actually my mind drifts as I try to recall any moments of joy I have actually experienced over the past seven days. Yes the sun in Scotland, although pleasantly brief, certainly contributed to my feelings of goodwill towards our time there. It seems that I always associate pleasant feelings with favourable weather. I wonder if I have 'seasonal affective disorder' – where one's mood is depressive, affected by the weather and shorter days of winter. Oh that isn't possible! While the weather has turned wintery in temperature and temperament, it is in fact the Northern Hemisphere's summer.

The villages, I recall, have been quaint and picturesque. The scenery has been lush and pretty and through all this my legs have just kept on turning and my brain has, when not completely blank, wandered haphazardly in a myriad of directions. I have had time to relive almost every other holiday and major experience over the period of our life as a couple. My thoughts have been filled of my children and wondering how they may be coping. I keep thinking of home as New Zealand, which is strangely odd as I haven't lived there for nine years. Maybe it is the combination of precipitation and greenery that flicks my thoughts to memories of my homeland. I have to keep reminding myself, that my reality is in fact life in a sunburnt country, where the greens are rarely any deeper than a eucalypt shade of sage. Maybe I am losing my mind? At other times the hours are automatically blocked out as soon as they tick by. This is not intentional – it is a bit like the mental numbness following childbirth, when endorphins have kicked in, to block out the pain. I am sure that this natural anaesthesia is what is keeping me going. The sheer exhaustion of each hill climb is forgotten quickly having accomplished the summit. The brain block allows my body a brief moment of recovery before it has to focus on the strength required for whatever the upcoming challenge.

I have begun swearing. I saw a program on TV last night called 'The F Word', about a cantankerous chef named Gordon Ramsay. If he can use that language on public television then the expletive seems to be the best verbal release from my demise. Every time I raise my head and look over Nev's shoulder and see another hill, it just slips out, and then again half way up when I glimpse again to see how far to summit, another slips, and then again at the top, exhausted and with a sense of relief, I look ahead only to find that there before us is another climb. 'Fuck!'

We have reached the point on the map where we rejoin the route we intended following earlier today. Not far along though we have a sense that something doesn't feel right and stop to consult the map again. We have made a stupid error. At the point of joining the lane we took a left fork instead of turning to the right, and are now heading toward Kings Meaburn, which we would have bypassed by now. Kings Meaburn is mentioned in our notes, but we would only have passed through it, if we had followed the guide from the morning direction. We are heading slightly away from our destination. This is very frustrating. We can't afford to make navigational errors and this is the second one today. We have no choice but to continue in this direction, as the map indicates that we can rectify our mistake by taking a road to the right in a couple of miles. Turning back now we would still be covering an additional four miles.

I wonder how two intelligent people, who have had some navigational experience over recent years, while participating in foot and mountain bike orienteering events, can both get directions wrong, especially at pedalling speed. It is safer to blame the environment rather than each other, and we decide it must be attributed to the lanes that are no wider than a driveway, and the signposts displaying only the next village, and we don't have all the villages on our map. Distances are rarely shown and we have seen few historic mile-stones markers for which I thought rural Britain was famous. In fact we stop to consult the map often. There is also just a little bit of doubt, that maybe when I transcribed from the original notes, that I may have reversed some of the directions. This happened to be the case when we missed the village of Glencoe a few days ago.

We really must make a concerted effort to keep moving so decide that Nev will remember the turns we must take, such as first right, second left. I will remember the names of the next few villages we are aiming for. We start pedalling and after only a couple of rotations Nev asks, "What is the name of that village again?"

"It's something like Meaburn" I reply, "no I think its two words. I can't actually remember." And even though the remembering of names is my responsibility, we have actually studied the map together, and neither can Nev remember, and so we stop and consult the map again. Today there are further complications such as heading in a direction towards villages that are similarly named, for example, Maulds Meaburn and Kings Meaburn. I feel rather anxious as I really am sure that I must be losing my marbles!

We have climbed into a wide empty expanse. The exposed area is of glistening wet rock interspersed with grassland, bracken and heath. I assume this must be what it is like to be on the moors but find later that we have just ridden through an upland area of limestone pavement called the Great Asby Scar.

The mobile phone rings, and in the time it takes to dismount and find it buried in the handlebar bag, the display shows we have missed a call from home. Our rummaging also shows that the handlebar bag has accumulated a puddle of water in the bottom. The paper, that we have been getting stamped each night to confirm ongoing accomplishment, and thus qualify us to purchase souvenir tee-shirts, is sodden. The water is lapping at the edges of our passports. Our valuables are rescued to the safety of a plastic bag. The weather has deteriorated further, even while we reorganise the stowage of our important items. Rain is now driving horizontally and in the exposed wind I am feeling wretched. I am cold, wet and hungry, but more than anything, I experience a deep yearning to be among home comforts and I want to talk to our son.

Outside the Orton pub 'Customers wanted, no experience required' is a sign too inviting to bypass. Our coats drip from hooks in the tiny porch as we tuck into hot soup and chips.

This isn't how it is supposed to be! We intended keeping our travel costs down by buying provisions and having picnic lunches each day. Spending £9 on a meagre quantity of food, eaten in pub warmth, has been a few moments of luxury that we have not factored into the budget.

Putting on a wet coat is one of the most miserable sensations that I know of. The collar, clammy around the neck, sends cold shivers down to sodden shoes. As we prepare to leave, a bunch of cyclists pull into the car park. The vehicle that parks alongside them is obviously their support van. Sign writing displays the charity that will benefit from the donations that this group from the British Police are fundraising for. They, like us, have also come from JOG. They are on road bikes without gear, and each day covering larger distances than us. Lancaster, about thirty miles away, is where they are heading today and I am envious of their confidence that this will be easily achievable. My envy extends to their obvious camaraderie, but more particularly of the soft option available to them, of travelling with a support vehicle that carries everything they need. We still have more than forty heavy miles to cover today. I don't know where I am going to get the strength from to accomplish today's mission.

The morsels at the pub hadn't filled us. We have only been riding for an hour and our stomachs are rumbling. At the pretty little village of Lowgill I ask the lady at the library if she knows of anywhere that we can shelter so that we can eat our packed lunch. She tells me she is not aware of any covered public place. I leave disappointed as I reckon in the same circumstances I would have shown some compassion, and invited wet waifs like us in, to drip in the building's lunch room. I would have fussed around making a hot cup of tea. Isn't that what the English are famous for? Maybe she thought that the moisture clinging to us would ruin the ancient tomes lining the walls, or maybe the one small room that she occupied was all that there was to the library?

The bus stop, walls and roof of stone, provides no warmth but at least it is shelter from the rain. Seated on the wooden bench we eat cheese and crackers washed down with lukewarm coffee from the flask.

The bus stop in Lowgill didn't offer much shelter

Drizzling rain continues to add misery to the day. At Casterton, on the outskirts of Kirkby Lonsdale we pull over to stretch our legs, outside a service station. I tell Nev that I am not going any further. Light is beginning to fade and it is already 5 o'clock.

"Check the map Nev, how far have we got to go? Thirty miles! You have got to be kidding?"

I'm insistent that we go no further. I know this appears irrational to Nev, and I also know that if I am not going any further, then I will need to resolve the immediate problems that are unfolding because of my autocratic decision.

I must look like a bedraggled old lady, well out of her comfort zone, as I drip over the service station floor, because the proprietor is being sympathetically kind. I am offered the use of her phone, then she helpfully seeks out a phone book and looks up the numbers that I will need to contact, to try and solve my dilemma. I know that I don't have the energy to continue the remaining thirty miles. Numerous phone calls establish that we can't hire a van, can't get into another closer Youth Hostel, and can't get a refund of the £31 we have already paid for the Slaidburn hostel; that I am quite convinced is an unachievable distance away.

The delay gives us another opportunity to carefully study the map and to reconfirm the distance that we have yet to cover. The map shows a lonely road; a thin black line threading through an expanse of white, interspersed with only the occasional wriggle of river blue and no other detail. The Forest of Bowland suggests vast isolation, with a desolate road running alongside Great Harlow, and with contours indicating that climbing was to continue.

Recollections of childhood television viewing, watching Sherlock Holmes and Dr Watson, out in the mist, on the moors, trying to solve mysteries while avoiding the sucking mud, comes to mind. There is no way I am continuing to an isolated destination in the wet weather, with light fading. The accumulation of eight days riding has physically taken its toll and my brain is telling me that to attempt completion of today's distance will put a toll, even bigger, on our relationship. I am not prepared to battle my physical exhaustion in order to defeat the negativity of my mental demons, no matter how much encouragement and cajoling is offered by my partner.

"Stop Nev, there's a B&B."

Nev pulls to the traffic island in the middle of the road.

"Don't you ever do that again!" he scolds.

"Do what?" I ask.

"Get off the bike in that way!"

In my opinion Nev had been about to ride from the safety of the central island, crossing the road lane towards the B&B, directly in front of a car that was coming towards us. I reckon Nev had misjudged and I was going to be road kill.

My accusatory explanation is thrown back at Nev as we proceed to walk across the road together. "I can't believe I leapt off, can't even remember doing it. I won't do it again; I'm surprised I'm standing here. I don't know how I did that. But don't put my life at risk - ever again."

The door is opened in answer to my knock and I blurt. "Have you got a room and how much? £60; okay we would like to take it, but more importantly are you able to help us get our gear dry, is there somewhere close we can get a takeaway tea, can we come back and eat it in your dining room?"

We present a sorry sight and our hosts are enormously helpful even though we must be the most demanding of guests. The heater is pumped up, wet gear taken from us, muddy drink bottles taken for sterilisation, plates put in the oven to warm.

We trudge up the stairway lugging the Carradice panniers, the brand used by British posties and reputably waterproof. We had, only a matter of weeks ago, imported them from the UK to Australia and brought them back again. Nev had offered to dissuade the doubt I expressed about them being waterproof, but never did demonstrate his intention to throw them into the swimming pool at home. I was reluctant to trust my gear, just to the supposed waterproof qualities of heavy canvas. I have too many memories of tramping in wet conditions in New Zealand carrying a canvas back-pack. Long weary days finished in a soggy sleeping bag.

Actually dare I say some of those hikes were before the time that plastic bags were a regular commodity? That makes me feel old! We had first come across plastic shopping bags - now the scourge of the 21st Century; and in South Australia now banned, - when we travelled in 1975 to the UK, with a stopover honeymoon in Hong Kong. In New Zealand, all of our goods were transported from store to home, in paper bags. In Hong Kong when we made purchases they were put into heavy-duty plastic bags and we arrived back at our hotel room with many of them.

The panniers are in fact sodden and significantly heavier than usual; no wonder we have been struggling with the extra weight created by the moisture.

Although we have no method of weighing the panniers to determine the exact increase in weight, it is clear as we heft them up the short flight of stairs, that they are heavier than usual. Fortunately our personal belongings have remained dry and secure in plastic rubbish bags that are sitting in a puddle of water. I am pleased that I insisted on using the extra protective layer.

Later that evening we talk of the Schapelle Corby scenario. Schapelle was arrested in October 2004 after being caught with 4.1 kg of marijuana in a boogie bag as she arrived at Bali airport. She had insisted on her innocence, when tried and charged in Bali for marijuana trafficking. Her main defence was that she had no idea that the boogie-board bag had increased in weight by 4.1 kilograms, and we questioned the merit of her explanation. I doubt our panniers had increased by anywhere near four kilograms however to us they were noticeably heavier.

While waiting at the 'chippy' we discuss our demise, having fallen well short of our intended day's route. It would be impossible for us to recover the miles we have not completed today. Even had we succeeded in arriving at Slaidburn, we knew we were going to have had a second day epic, with 80 miles also to be completed tomorrow.

"One hundred and twenty miles in one day to catch up; don't even try to convince me that it is achievable" I warn Nev. "It is not going to happen; even if we are going to follow the effort with two nights in Chester; and our only rest day."

Warmth envelopes the room and, together with the peace of having reached a solution that, on our host's recommendation; tomorrow we would do a catch up and travel to Chester by train; sleep easily overcomes the exhaustion.

There is a feeling of déjà vu around the decision to have a slight abandonment. In the same district, back in the summer of 1977 we had been about to return to New Zealand via six months further travel in America. First though, we decided that a quick tour of the United Kingdom was required. London had been our home on and off for eighteen months, but apart from an Easter spent in Cornwall, we had seen little of the 'mother country'. Having already sold the VW Combi van that had been our transport and home in Europe, we purchased a 1963 Mini Minor car and minimalist two-man pup tent, for our UK expedition. Beautiful summer days in Scotland had been followed by a few days of wet camping whilst in the Lake District. The 'last straw', leading to the decision to abandon that trip, was the improvised use of the vehicle, because of the lack of any other shelter or 'cook-house'. While I was sitting in the front driver's seat of the Mini, to stay dry, I was cooking our dinner; pot balanced on the single-burner gas stove that was placed on the floor on the left side, in the passenger's foot space.

Day Eight Stats:

Nev's cycle computer drowned today therefore estimation of distance covered 103.8 kilometres, 64.52 miles

Trip Miles total no longer able to be recorded as my Speedo drowned at 480.30 miles

Kirkby Lonsdale – Chester

Day Nine: UK
Thursday, 14th June

Calmness pervades on waking as there is no need to rush this morning. A full English breakfast is being cooked for us. I am trying to ignore the drizzle outside yet it is threatening to dampen my spirits. I am in no hurry to put on my soggy shoes and leave this homely comfort.

Our hosts assure us that the nineteen mile ride to Lancaster will be a gentle downhill along minor roads. It is exactly that. We need an easy day. I am deeply weary and Nev is still having problems with his knee. The knee is a sore point that we don't talk about much, but now and again Nev mentions that the pain is niggling him. Never one to complain, and particularly less inclined to do so when he views the situation as having no option but to 'soldier on'; I have to admire his tenacity.

The countryside is as pretty as a chocolate-box picture; stone walls secure stone farmhouses that nestle amongst the vivid greens of well nourished woods and trees. Pastures, long and thick, are yearning for animals to reduce their growth. The gentle decline creates natural acceleration. Despite the drizzle my mood lifts. There is no time pressure today as trains depart Lancaster to Chester every half hour.

Feeling relaxed in city traffic is always difficult for me and today I am particularly tense as we negotiate large roundabouts, one way systems and have to stay clear of screaming emergency vehicles. It's a pleasure to pull into the railway station and secure the tandem to a pole. Tickets are booked on the 1.29 p.m. to Chester and the tandem is left at the station allowing us an unencumbered exploration on foot, of Lancaster in drizzle. Cities don't hold our interest for long. There is little point looking at shopping precincts, as apart from small amounts of food, we are unable to carry purchases. After a cursory wander past the castle and cathedral we consider we have done the sights justice and return to the station.

This is to be our first experience travelling by train without the tandem disguised in packaging. The platform official had indicated we might have a problem fitting the tandem on. That is Nev's domain while I manage our six small items of luggage, no easy matter when one has only two arms. Boarding the train is the rush we expect. Trains stop for only a few minutes. In such a small time-frame we have to scan the incoming carriages to identify the bicycle logo that indicates bikes can travel in that compartment. Nev, while pushing the tandem, runs in the direction of that carriage. I grab all of our baggage and with one almighty heave, hoist our gear into the carriage that stops nearest to me. Within a split second of clambering into the carriage the train begins moving. We have boarded on separate carriages and Nev makes his way to join me.

Watching the miles pass by at great speed, confirms for me how impossible it would have been to cycle this distance. I'm deep in distant thoughts as we wait for the announcement of the station that is to be our connection to Chester. Above the clattering of the train I hear the short, sharp, broadcast of three words announcing the next station. The first word starts with 'W'. My elbow nudges Nev into action.

"Quick, that's us," I prompt.

Nev runs to the rear carriage to retrieve the tandem. I grab the bags and wait by the door. The train stops. I'm off. Nev joins me on the platform. The train has already moved on. I look up at the station signage and see Wigan Western Line.

"Oh shit!"

The platform official walks towards us.

"You aren't supposed to be here are you?"

"We were supposed to be at Warrington Quay Head; how did you know?"

The official explains that they are informed when to expect bikes. Warrington Quay Head, first name starting with 'W' and made up of two other words is two stations further down the track. He assures us that catching another train to Warrington Quay Head won't be a problem; however it does mean a delay at Wigan Western Line.

Thirty minutes later we are again perched at the platform edge, ready to run if necessary to catch a carriage. No worries! We alight two stations later at Warrington Quay Head.

The afternoon is now dragging on as there is now a further forty minute wait for the Chester connection. Never mind that we could have been relaxing in Chester by now. At least we are seated on a bench rather than cycle seat, and beside, rather than behind each other, and our legs are relaxed rather than turning constantly. Fortunately the English are prepared for cool summer days. The heating in the little waiting room at Warrington is welcome, as we have again spent the entire day in damp clothes and wet shoes. Time passes quickly as I am eaves-dropping on the drivel of conversation between an older couple. Their friendship appears clandestine. They speak of illness symptoms, and other private issues, all the while nipping from a shared drinking flask. That their voices become much too loud for the whispered conversation they think they are having, indicates they are becoming a little inebriated.

Our skills must be improving as we catch the train easily. With the announcement that we are approaching Chester, preparations begin for our third rush from a train this afternoon. The disembarkation is without mishap and we have been able to navigate the route, extremely straight forward actually, to the Youth Hostel.

The door is opened by a child and I notice six other children rushing through the foyer and up the stairs on the left. There are other children scurrying down the basement stairway; in fact children are everywhere. I am beginning to wonder if we dreamt our way from Thomas the Tank Engine to Old Mother Hubbard.

"It's the end of the school year," the desk attendant informs us, "and many schools use the Youth Hostels as school camps. There are thirty-five children in residence. I recommend in the morning, come down for breakfast at nine; the children will have left for their day trip by then".

"Great!" I mumble under my breath.

What better way to start a rest period than to catch up with the laundry. Our wet clothing is soon hanging in the drying room. It will have two entire nights and a day in between to dry. It will be fresh and crisp and warm when next I put it on. Chores completed it is now time to revive in the hot shower. An uninspiring frozen microwave dinner purchased from a deli about a mile walk away makes a less than satisfying tea. At least our third floor room, accessed only by stairs, is private. I make a concerted effort to check out where the fire exit is and then lie on the bottom bunk. For the first time on this trip, I allow myself to think about tomorrow. The prospect of a day off is wonderful.

Day Nine Stats:

The day we cheated!

Estimated distance covered 32.5 kilometres, 20.3 miles by tandem

By train: about 78 miles

Chester

Day Ten: UK
Friday, 15ᵗʰ June

All night long, rain fell. I know it rained all night because I lay in the bottom bunk fretfully listening to it! A few hours of deep sleep had been interrupted by Nev's snoring. Wood slats on the bunk pressed through the thin mattress. The sheet bag, compulsory bed linen supplied by every Youth Hostel – I believe to avoid scabies infestations - twisted to thwart my tossing and turning, as the sheet gripped the plastic mattress cover. I am beginning to get annoyed, and that emotion disturbs my resting brain. Okay, may as well get up and use the bathroom! The night calm is constantly interrupted by the thumps and crashes of entries and exits, into and out of the adjoining rooms. At 6 a.m. I hear the whispers of children, I expect the queue on their lower floor encourages them to sneak up to our top level bathroom. The heavy rain has found a weak point, and drips through the ceiling with a spatter-spatter, as drops bounce in the puddle now pooling on the carpet outside of our room. I lie uneasily, waiting for the daylight to indicate a civilised start time to my one and only rest day on this trip.

Nev has been keen for me to see Chester, a town that he had visited back in 1999. In that year, he had travelled to the UK with the intention of finding work, either in Britain or Europe, as a computer programmer. He was experienced in COBOL, an ancient software language that had used a two digit code for numbers. There was widespread concern that rolling from '99, into the 21st Century, the double zero digits would nullify processes and cause a viral attack by the Millennium Bug! It was anticipated that this bug could, in the worst case scenario, stall much of the public infrastructure now operated by computers. Although Nev found work in Belgium, it never actually eventuated, largely because of the difficulty in trying to gain a work visa as an older person. Sadly he was a fifth generation New Zealander, as was I; a claim we would usually be proud of. Unfortunately because of the longevity of this inherited citizenship, he did not qualify under the British or European Union grandparent entry qualifications.

Nev was 'spot-on' to choose Chester as the venue for our day off, even though it is, both in time and distance, greater than half way through the journey. We register for a morning guided-tour and are pleased to see that the dull weather has kept other tourists away, so we have the guide to ourselves. Much of the city's 2000 year history is contained within the historic stone walls, and easily reached by walking from one point of interest to another. The architecture, particularly of the 700 year old 'The Rows', now the main shopping precinct, provides an interesting facade to the many ancient Roman ruins hidden in the basements. We cover an enormous time-span in history that is as fascinating as it is enjoyable. At the end of the tour, our guide asks us for feedback, as she had been thinking of giving up guiding. She is from

Eastern Europe and, because of her birthplace, felt she may not be suitably qualified. We assured her that it didn't matter to us that she was not born in the UK as she was obviously very passionate and knowledgeable about her subject.

Following the guided tour notes we have been given we continue to explore on our own, and then walk back to the hostel late in the afternoon. In our room, I lie on the bottom bunk, intending just to rest; but fall into a sound sleep. Nev wakes me after an hour to join him to get some dinner. Having walked today for six hours, we have effectively replaced the same period of time that we would usually have spent on the bike, but with 'striding' rather than 'rotating' legs.

Day Ten Stats:

No cycling at all, Yah Hoo!

Chester – Clun

Day Eleven: UK
Saturday, 16th June

Protected from the moisture, in raincoat and leggings, we set off. The weather forecast is for scattered showers, yet we are already experiencing a rather heavy and persistent morning downpour as we ride under the only cloud in the sky! The cloud is hovering directly above us like an oversized 'zeppelin'; silver lined as the sun bursts beyond it. The 'zeppelin' explodes and the watery deluge crashes down! We are desperate to escape the 'rain-radar' that has obviously spied us, and to be able to gain the solar blanket of a clear sky. For the entire morning we have the misfortune of cycling beneath this rain cloud! It is travelling in the same direction as us, and obviously at the same speed. We hail a couple of cyclists coming from the South. They too have been travelling all morning but unlike us are noticeably dry! The fine weather is in their favour but apparently determined to elude us.

Moments wash into oblivion as we journey through the day. There is little of cheer to record. We cross the border into Wales. The countryside is picture-perfect except that the profusion of vibrant greens is washed-out by grey weather. Wet roads, drizzle and passing through the many puddles, blur into damp memories.

At mid-day, we are faced again with the difficulty of finding somewhere dry to sit and eat the food we are carrying. The locals at Ellesmere can't offer any advice as to where we can eat and be dry, unless we purchase food at a nearby café. Through luck, as we ride around the block, we notice a building with a large number of people entering, and from which emanate the sounds of gaiety. We decide to investigate, and following the sounds, happen upon the village weekly market in full swing. We wander amongst stalls of local produce, passing without sampling the local ciders and 'real ales' with wonderful names such as 'Foxes Nob' and 'Piddle Hole'. A wooden pallet, tucked away, but giving us full view of the hubbub, provides a good vantage of the providores, and a quiet dry corner where we sit to eat our bread and cheese.

We have only travelled ten miles further when the 'hunger growls' are with us again. Passing through Baschurch, there is a churchyard on our left with a portico that looks like an ideal shelter. The wooden bench seat, fitted to the stone wall, is dry; an ideal place to sit, assemble and eat our sandwiches. The portico is a memorial to a woman whose Christian names were Margaret Adelaide. It seems fortuitous that we would find shelter beneath a name familiar to us; Adelaide being our hometown.

In spite of the weather, this is a reasonably easy day in terms of cycling effort. There has been only one stage that we felt, on reflection, we could have navigated differently. As 'doing as directed' is apparently a trait in both of our natures, we have chosen a route that we feel we should never deviate from. This meant that today, we left a well surfaced road, to defer to a quiet secondary one which then led into minor lanes. In effect we had left a road, going in much the same direction we needed to be heading and that had allowed us a good pace, only to change it for the smaller lanes which meant we were faced with extra effort, and the slowness caused by the steep 'ups-and-downs'! These reflections must be disregarded, so that we can feel good about adhering to our self-made rules. Rigorously following the precise set of directions has been of more importance to us than our own comfort. Clearly we need to have a more relaxed and flexible attitude!

My perspective of the countryside has become limited, because Nev's back and shoulders, with helmeted head, fill the narrow lanes that are bordered by hedgerows. Some hedgerows extend up to three meters in height, with the occasional taller tree branches reaching out to touch the shrubbery opposite and threatening at times to block out the sky completely!

Arriving at the village of Clun by 5.30 p.m., we decide should be rewarded with the well deserved treat of a pub meal, a few ales, and some socialising with the locals. We anticipate this will be a great way to fill a couple of hours, before retiring to the bed and breakfast, (reportedly only another two miles) south of Clun. We don't expect to have the hotel dining-room to ourselves, as only a week ago in Scotland, the locals were all eating at 5:00 p.m. Shropshire locals however, must be much more in-tune with us, having a mealtime pattern much like ours. The Sun Inn doesn't open until 6.00 p.m. and the Buffalo Inn, where we are intending to have a drink, doesn't serve meals until 6:30! Nev phones Tyndings Bed and Breakfast to let them know we are definitely coming, just delaying our arrival, waiting to order our evening meal. The B&B proprietors offer to cook for us, so there is no reason to dally. We decide to imbibe in one pint of ale though, to sustain us for the remaining two miles.

I think Nev went up to the bar and asked the barman, "One for the lady with the highest alcohol content." The trickle of alcohol flows down through my body – unusually not to my bladder – to pool in my lower legs, which instantly become jelly-like. A charge of contentment then rushes to fill my dehydrated cells, and slowly oozes into the brain cavity. So, in this slightly inebriated state, I claim my back seat throne. Good spirits prevail, even as we stand on the main village road, looking at the hill before us that appears to be rising directly from the village main street. We are not in the least bit daunted by the fact that this hill seems to be climbing vertically towards heaven.

Really steep; is an understatement of the incline. We attack the climb with renewed vigour, and with powerful pedal strokes, push the beast higher and higher.

"I'll tell you a joke" Nev says, "It'll take your mind off the effort. A tandem rider is stopped by a police car. What've I done, officer? asks the rider. Perhaps you didn't notice sir, but your wife fell off your bike half a mile back. Oh, thank God for that, says the rider - I thought I'd gone deaf!" It's not that funny, but my tittering turns to laughter. The laughter triggers an unexpected emotion. Suddenly, simultaneously laughing and sobbing, hysteria threatens to overwhelm me. Laughter catches at the back of my throat and tears stream down my cheeks. Nev pulls to the side of the road. "Come on girl, pull yourself together" Nev prompts.

I struggle to gain some semblance of control, trying to think calm thoughts to quell the hysterics. My legs are wobbling and I have to give in to their trembling as there is no way they will have the strength to continue rotating those pedals. I choose to walk but Nev reckons it is easier to ride rather than walk and push the tandem, so he pedals alone for the final few hundred meters to Tyndings Bed & Breakfast.

Janet & Hugh Quan welcome a solo tandem rider and a puffy eyed walker to their beautiful home, a 250 year old stone cottage. Narrow twisting stairs lead us to a quaint loft-room, decorated in linen and lace, with sparkling dragonfly lights adorning the beamed ceiling. There is no ensuite, but it is only a short flight of stairs down to our private hot shower. A delicious home-cooked dinner, including dessert, eaten while listening to soothing melodies sung by Vera Lyn, makes for a relaxing evening in this pretty rural setting.

Day Eleven Stats:

Estimated distance covered: 116.03 kilometres, 72.1 miles

Trip Miles total has been assessed at: 590.13

Clun - Welsh Bicknor

Day Twelve: UK
Sunday, 17th June

Wha a relief to wake to a fine warm day. We have been approaching each day cautiously now, because we are unsure what we are going to face in terms of weather, distance or terrain. This morning is pleasant, the sun shines, and the road is mostly flat, or even slightly descending. The Shropshire hills provide a pretty vista of lush green fields, each clearly defined by dark emerald hedges. We are setting a good pace and feeling buoyant and relaxed, having covered the first ten miles quickly. Our reward for our good progress will be a long stop at Wigmore.

I can't believe that I am complaining, as we begin the short walk in the direction of Wigmore Castle ruins, but the sun is hot and the gradient, while slight, is steep enough for my leg muscles to indicate that they are extremely tired. We agree that in spite of the walking effort using our leg muscles in a slightly different manner to cycling, it is still a strain and the prospect of continuing even a small climb up to the ruins, is unappealing. Instead we return to St Paternus Church where we have parked the tandem, for a morning snack and to wander amongst the tombstones, erected in the mid 1800s.

It is a sunny Sunday and back on the bike we are distracted from our own efforts by watching a number of other people on the opposite side of the road, participating in their sport and enjoying the weather. First there is a group of individuals cycling in what appears to be a short-course cycle race. Later on, in the distance there is another cyclist heading towards us and we take an even keener interest when we notice that it is actually two cyclists on a tandem, followed closely by another. They keep on coming and we count twelve in all. There is always a male in the captain position, leading female stokers. I reckon the average age of the riders would be somewhere in the 70's!

"Nev I know now why I haven't gotten on so well with this tandem experience. I reckon I'm much too young to appreciate this method of travel," I joke with Nev as they pass. Nev though, must have been aware of the benefit of being an older captain. He has decided not to shave whilst on this trip, and the grey whiskers, sprouting from his upper lip and chin, I consider extremely unattractive, and think they have aged him at least ten years!

Hampton Court Castle in Herefordshire, just south of Leominster, is our perfectly timed lunch stop at around 1.30 p.m. There is a garden here open for public viewing and we park the tandem against a tree amongst the other parked vehicles. This is the twelfth day of our journey and the first opportunity that we have had to 'fire-up' the little Pocket-Rocket gas stove that we have been carrying. Hot soup and brewed coffee is ready in minutes, providing the lunch time sustenance that we had expected would refuel our bodies every day. Swallows, flitting and darting across the expanse of lawn, provide light entertainment against the grand stone backdrop of turrets, towers and arched windows, that make up the 15th Century castle.

My view

The day continues pleasantly, with favourable cycling conditions, apart from dodging the deep puddles that have formed in the lanes, and one short but tough hill-climb, just before the town of Ross-on-Wye.

Following the B4234 we travel beyond Ross-on-Wye, until we are riding parallel with the Wye River. We establish that we have a half mile or so to go, as we simply take a footbridge, crossing to Welsh Bicknor and the Youth Hostel. There is a pub on our left and the decision is unanimous to celebrate a good day with a pint of good ale. The late afternoon temperature is pleasant enough to sit outside beside the river, sipping and congratulating ourselves on our conquests to date. Thus relaxed we delay the final stage of our day's journey, so that we will arrive at the Youth Hostel in good time to prepare dinner. It is after all almost within sight, across and only a little further up the river.

Subsequently about a mile into a steep uphill section, the liquor, having been thoroughly absorbed by my leg muscles - turning them to a quivering jelly – now travels vein-wards to my brain. This truly is a steep hill, at least 10%, and it's an enormous effort to be strong and focus on achieving the summit. My attention moves towards the hazy niggling that is in my brain telling me that the direction we are travelling doesn't feel right! Moving away from the river doesn't seem conducive to the fact that we have still to cross a bridge. No bridge came into view when we were beside the river, and I am worried that we must have missed it. The first house that comes into view, after the top of the climb, is on the edge of the village of Lydbrook which is not featured in our notes at all. We stop to ask for directions. Sure enough, the gentleman confirms our fears, directing us downward; indicating that we will need to go all the way back to the bottom of the hill, before the Youth Hostel across the river will come into view. In spite of staring to the left, as we retrace our trail, slowing at every little track heading towards the river, we still cannot find an obvious path leading towards a bridge. Having now descended all the way back to our starting point, we decide to phone the hostel.

"What are you doing on that side of the river?" the warden asks. "No-one ever comes from that direction. You won't find the bridge. It was unsafe and has been shut-down for a long time."

In response to my request for directions to the hostel he queries "Directions to the hostel? You will need to ride back in the direction you have come, as far as Kerne Bridge, that's the only crossing in this area. Cross the river there, and then take the first left. It's about six miles."

Our anticipated late afternoon arrival time has now deteriorated to be a weary early evening one. The sky has darkened with the threat of rain. Fortunately the warden offers to come in his van to pick us up. We strip the tandem of bags and wheels so that it will fit in his little Citroen. While 'taxiing us' the warden comments "I hope you are self-catering, as a school group has just left this afternoon and they have eaten the entire stock of food?"

Luckily we have dinner supplies and the warden assures us that he will be at the supermarket well before he starts his shift tomorrow at 7.00 a.m. We will then be able to buy the breakfast provisions which we do need.

We are delivered at the Victorian rectory that is the Welsh Bicknor Youth Hostel, situated on the bank of the Wye River, just in time to miss a soaking from the rain, that we are told has 'set in' for the coming week.

Day Twelve Stats:

Estimated distance covered: 94.14 kilometres, 58.5 miles

Trip Miles total: Assessed at 648.63

Welsh Bicknor – Cheddar

Day Thirteen: UK
Monday, 18th June

I t had been a real hassle the previous day getting to Welsh Bicknor, and I was so thankful for the ride offered by the hostel manager; that small trip was a leg-saver. Yesterday, trying to follow the guide notes to the 'nth degree, was our downfall. We need to be more flexible. With last evening's rescue fresh in our minds, we seriously consider the guide details, offering two different route choices as far as Chepstow. Not long into studying the scenic route, we are presented with the following description; *'Follow river along bridle path; (not very nice according to one report) Follow footpath (Cyclists are asked to dismount and walk). Come to stile & gate. At Hadnock Court pick up minor road. Right A4136 Left at Junction'*. Dismount! Style! Clearly this route is not an option.

Route Two is equally daunting, particularly as directions are preceded with a bold text heading of 'The High Road'. The map shows this Welsh Bicknor Youth Hostel is tucked between the Wye River, and a densely wooded area. Although there are no contours visible, the lack of urbanisation implies climbing. For us this second route is already thwarted. We are well aware that there is no longer a bridge, and the first direction is to cross the river.

We know from our van ride down to the hostel the previous evening, that there is now a long uphill ride on the narrow gravel surface driveway, to get out of this incredibly steep valley. Facing such a significant challenge as soon as we mount, does not appeal to me today. I ask some German travellers, if I can join them to travel in their car to the gateway that stands at the entrance to the property. This turns out to be a highly exciting ride as the car seeks traction in the wet gravel surface, skidding around the hairpin, uphill gradients, on some of the corners.

I have no feelings of remorse at leaving Nev to 'slog the climb' alone. Not to be defeated, or feel like he is cheating, I reckon he is happy to accept the challenge. I rejoin him at the top of the drive and we continue together to climb gradually up to the village of Marstow.

Choosing from either of the routes recommended in the guide had been difficult, as each threatened to be challenging both navigationally and physically, at least for the first couple of hours. So, for the moment, we decide to give up on scenic routes, and just for a little while, as far as Monmouth, deviate completely away from the notes, succumbing to the temptation of the wide green line that, represents the A40.

Initially the sealed verge offers a semblance of comfort, and any feelings of apprehension, as we hug the border of the three lane motorway, are dispelled, soothed by the gentle downhill gradient that makes riding favourable. We are quietly confident that this is a good choice.

The drizzle arrives simultaneously with the disappearance of the security of the sealed verge! We are now sharing the motorway and are at the mercy of the heavy traffic hurrying towards Exeter. This feels like a game of Russian roulette. With the traffic bearing down upon us from behind, the swoosh of rubber tyres flicking up sprays of water is making it difficult to trust that the overtaking vehicles will ease into the centre lane and leave us with enough room in the left lane. I sit on the back seat of the bike, legs 'twirling', eyes shut tight, in an effort to block out the reality, and saying (in my head, because I know Nev would not put up with such nonsense) *'please take me home to my babies.'* But I don't think my children - as eighteen and twenty year olds - would appreciate their mother's anxiety either. Up until this point in life, I have never given my own death any thought, but now I have decided that I am not yet prepared to leave the world, and being flattened by a juggernaut is not the way I want to go. After five miles of anxious riding we leave the A40 and, on the outskirts of Monmouth, take the less busy B4293, together vowing that, no matter what, we will never cycle another 'A' road.

Monmouth is only a small town, but we are finding it difficult to navigate through, as we cannot locate the River Wye, from which to get our bearings. A pedestrian, holding a map, seems the obvious person to approach for directions, so we ask how to get to Chepstow. He explains that the Chepstow Road is the most direct route, and in all seriousness, then adds; "As you are on a cycle the hills won't bother you."

How stupid can some people be? What a ridiculous comment! We obviously have no intention of taking his advice; instead we choose to follow the slightly longer route, along Redbrook Road, following the beautiful Wye valley.

What bliss it is to travel quickly and effortlessly providing relief for our aching knees. Though our moment of enjoyment, as seems usual on this trip, is short lived. A torrential rain storm envelopes us; considerably reducing our visibility, as our faces are being bombarded with pellet sized rain drops, and we squint to protect our eyes. Stopping to avoid the worst of the onslaught; while still seated on the bike, we clutch at the grasses growing along the edge of a steep roadside bank. Leaning on an angle into the shrubbery provides us an umbrella-like shelter.

Today we have made sandwiches for lunch. There is a welcome break in the rain as we approach a roadside lay-by. There is no shelter or picnic-table and bench, but it's a convenient time to stop for revitalising, both from our nutritious sustenance, and from the emotional uplift that a phone call to our offspring will bring. Chelsea has returned to Adelaide from a trip to Bali and we are keen to hear about her holiday.

Back on the move again good spirits prevail as we each relay our individual telephone conversations with our daughter.

This afternoon we are heading for Cheddar. I have happy memories of a day trip from London to Cheddar, by bus, with New Zealand and Australian friends, back in 1976. It was my introduction to Scrumpy, 'real' cider, and I have a stone jug with 'Oi've just cum up from Zummerzet' adorning my kitchen, atop the cupboards, along with the Grecian urn and brightly painted Mexican tray; souvenirs of other travels. I can't remember much of 'the gorge' but I do remember Wookey Hole, probably because of photographs taken at the time.

First we have to cross the Mouth of the Severn, by the Severn Bridge, a four-lane toll bridge; free to cyclists and travellers from Wales. The bridge is an enormous structure of 1,600 metres in length. The cycle-way on the outer edge is exposed to the cross-wind that threatens to blow us into the bridge's security fence. As we climb to the apex, we realise the significance of the span height and length; it has been quite an effort, fortunately followed by zooming down the exact equivalent distance on the English side.

It is our intention to avoid Bristol, by following the cycle-way through Pill, to Clapton-in-Gordano; however the metropolitan area seems to extend infinitum. This cycle-path gives more frustration with far too many barriers. The barriers are erected to slow bikes down, but they always become entrapment for us, because of the length of our tandem.

There is a vicious easterly head-wind, and it is a pleasure to turn out of it, yet each time we do, we both groan at the sight of the Severn Bridge. "There's that bloody bridge again!" Nev points out the obvious as it always seems to be directly ahead of us! The enormity of its span gives us the sense that we have made no progress, both because it is always so close, and because we are facing it, riding in a direction opposite to that which we need to be travelling.

The pathway takes us beside smelly, stagnant, canals; glass strewn industrial estates, and skirts the perimeter of an enormous parking area where new cars are stored while waiting to be transported. We have a strong sense that we are cycling in circles that are becoming wider, but are not taking us in the direction we want to be heading. Nev vents his frustration with lots of muttered comments that I can't hear clearly and, because they might be directed at me, I am not going to seek clarification of. My own annoyance sets into a solid silence, particularly as, on consulting the map, we find we are almost on the west coast. We are now passing through Weston-in-Gordano, then after a couple of miles, pass through Walton-in-Gordano; both towns to the south-west of, and by-passing Clapton-in-Gordano, where we are supposed to be heading towards, clearly confirming that we have gone astray. The error is easily recovered, as the route, even though out of the way, is still in the general direction that we want to be travelling. It doesn't seem to matter that the error can be corrected; irritation has now become lodged; to scratch 'like a sharp grass seed in a running sock'.

"Curse those cycle paths," Nev exclaims. "We have been circling around, miles out of our way to avoid traffic on city roads. I ride in a city every day, I'm not fazed by the traffic and we should have had a much more direct route!"

We are disappointed, because today was to be one of our easier days and certainly one of the shortest in terms of distance. We are frozen in icy silence, because of our different views of what constitutes realistic route choice; Nev comfortable with city roads and traffic, me preferring the quieter option of a cycle-way. This is now going to be a long day, due to the extra distance, as we meandered on the cycle path, caused by what can essentially be considered my poor navigation. Intermittent drenching from developing rain showers compounds the 'cool' silence.

Travelling is slow this afternoon, as the cycling is uphill, followed by uphill, repetitively for much of the time. I feel tightness in my chest that I dismiss as just my vivid imagination. I am sure that sore arms usually signal that a heart attack is imminent, and I don't have those symptoms, so I ignore the pressure I feel. On the next hill though I have the same sensation, so I say to Nev "Just thought I'd let you know that I have a tightness in my chest. I really think it is nothing, but thought I should let you know, so that if I drop dead in the night, you will remember this conversation."

"Oh come on Lou, you can't cark-it now, we only have two days to go!"

Nev's pragmatic response is what I should have expected, but I am weighed down by negativity, so replaying it in my head, I am looking for just a small glimmer of loving concern. Somehow, if there was any, I think I missed it. It sets me to thinking of another time, when we were celebrating our 25th Wedding Anniversary with friends, and Nev was asked; "What does it take to be married for such a long time?"

His response was "Well; put it this way. Once I have started something; I never give up on it."

I considered that comment hurtful at the time, but here we are still together, after thirty-one years of matrimony, travelling in the same direction, mutually determined that we are not going to give-up this journey that we started together. I need to focus on being grateful; I guess we have the same philosophy, even though we express it differently.

By the time we get to Yatton we figure that we have about nine and a half miles; perhaps an hour more, to travel today. With energy levels depleted we break the final attack into quarters. This seems rather pathetic, but we figure that focusing on a fifteen minute goal should be achievable. Counting down the minutes is as slow as watching water coming to the boil, but I am determined not to exceed the quarter hour time spans. The stop is brief; a quick dismount, a couple of squats, stretch and shake of the legs, and within minutes, with backside seated, we launch on the next attack. All goes well for about ten pedal rotations and then both my legs scream as if the muscles are being seared by red hot pokers.

I groan aloud "Oh, ouch!"

Nev chuckles through the headphones, yet is simultaneously groaning with me. I cannot believe the pain, and he explains that he too has been caught by the lactic acid burn. This brief, intensely painful phenomenon catches us unawares within the first few seconds, every time we restart from a break, throughout the rest of the trip.

It is late afternoon when we finally arrive at the Cheddar Gorge Youth Hostel. This is the best hostel room to date, with two beds and tiny ensuite bathroom. I had hoped to visit the geographical attractions of Cheddar Gorge and possibly Wookey Hole, but while consulting tourist brochures over dinner, I find that the gorge is about two miles out of Cheddar, and not in the direction that we will be travelling tomorrow. There is no point feeling morose. I comfort myself with a fat-fortifying dinner of Fish and Chips, accompanied by the delicious vegetable serving of the British invention of bright green 'mushy peas'. I remind myself that when we visited this area thirty or so years ago, it had been a brief glimpse of a very attractive waterfall that we had captured forever on a Kodak slide. The picture was also a reminder of our disappointment at the time, that there was an entrance fee to view the natural phenomena. Having come from New Zealand, our homeland then, easily accessible natural attractions were always free to visitors.

Day Thirteen Stats:

Estimated distance covered: 122.30 kilometres, 76 miles

Trip Miles total: Assessed at 724.63

Cheddar – Okehampton

Day Fourteen: UK
Tuesday, 19th June

Although a mere four miles return trip, this morning the additional ride out to Cheddar Gorge is not an option. The B3151 is our route choice. It will take us as far as Wedmore where we will then join the A39 briefly. The remainder of the day will be on minor roads, taking us in a more or less south-westerly direction, through Somerset to Okehampton in Devon.

In spite of the prospect of having a journey of eighty miles before us, I have a good feeling about today. The morning air is dry and the sun is weakly attempting to shine. A cacophony of musical twitters comes from the tall hedgerows but the symphony is constantly interrupted by those short little repetitive breaths in my ear. Nev has been my conjoined companion; ahead of me on the bike, beside in bed, or more often above on the top bunk, for the past thirteen days and right now, I have the most intense desire to be alone. I reach forward and, as I flick the intercom switch to off, blissful isolation is achieved. I feel just a little sneaky during the process, but enjoy having just the bird tunes to accompany my thoughts.

Gaps between speaking had often been long, but it is at least thirty minutes before I hear Nev ask

"Are you still there Lou?"

This has been asked at other times, and always makes me smile, as I have nowhere to go! My mischievous interlude is over, as I reach forward guiltily and switch on our communication link. I am feeling just a little self-satisfied though, as I reckon having taken that long for Nev to miss me, this must confirm that he can't usually hear me breathing!

My feeling of euphoria is short lived, as drizzle soon descends, indicating we are about to experience our seventh consecutive day of rain. The precipitation puts a damper over my earlier enthusiasm. I have suddenly completely lost interest. I hate the rain, I hate the bike, and I hate cycling! I know though, that if I just keep on pushing my legs around, we will eventually arrive at our destination, and the day will draw to an end. I just want to get today over with, so that I can feel excited about having only two more days to go.

Having had the tourist pamphlet whipped out of my hands on our second day, I have never felt confident about snapping photos while 'in motion'. Today photo opportunities are by-passed. Neither of us wants the brief interlude of stopping, to take a snapshot, to be followed by the excruciating pain of 'lactic acid burn'. Besides, the photos would just reflect the dismal weather conditions.

Ahead we can see a lone cow crossing the road. As we near the animal, we slow down to proceed cautiously. A farmer steps from a gateway to our left. Casting a quick glance in our direction, he halts our approach as he walks out directly in front of us, holding a limp piece of orange rope at waist height. This he drags across the lane and attaches to a post on the other side. This barrier, though fragile, gives us no option but to stop and wait in the drizzle, astride the bike, while streams of watery mud, now mixing with excrement, swirls in pools around our feet, as the cows move from the field, and cross the lane, to the farmer's milking shed.

We have seen little in the way of traffic today, but this obstruction causes a line of vehicles, including a bus, to queue opposite, facing towards us. How such a line of vehicles happens to appear in such a short time, in the middle of nowhere is unbelievable. The farmer duly removes his rope, allowing the procession of vehicles opposite to start moving forward. Being the minor vehicle on this occasion is a clear disadvantage, so we wait a little longer to let the traffic pass on by. By the time the convoy passes, we are splattered with a messy mixture of mud and cow shit, up to our knees.

A rather messy halt to our progress

The conclusion to the cycling day is a struggle up the steep hill that leads into Okehampton, then conquering Station Road that is an even steeper incline.

Finally, dragging our bodies, with gear in hand, we install ourselves in the upstairs room at the guest house. A large room with double bed, superb hot shower followed by a hot pub meal, barely numbs the weariness.

I have almost blocked out this entire day, damped it down like sodden ashes never to spark even in reminiscing. I am going to bed tonight, as usual deliberately oblivious to the journey we are to face tomorrow. The prospect of only two more days to go is still too daunting to look forward to with any enthusiasm.

Day Fourteen Stats:

Estimated distance covered: 125.5 kilometres, 78 miles

Trip Miles total: Assessed at 802.63

Okehampton - St Austell

Day Fifteen: UK
Wednesday, 20th June

Our hosts at the Meadowlea Guest House in Okehampton, ask what it is like to ride the tandem in the wind? Nev replies, "apart from one afternoon in Scotland, we haven't had any strong winds to contend with."

We should have gleaned a hint of what we may encounter today, when our hosts look at each other in a quizzical way, with eyebrows slightly raised, but say nothing.

Okehampton sits at an altitude of 1020 feet and because of this I logically deduce that, as St Austell is on the Cornish coast, we must now go down to sea level. There is however a recent memory nagging at my brain, as I recall what I had heard from other cyclists we had encountered along the way. Whenever we spoke of Scottish highland passes, they had responded with comments such as 'Wait till you get to Cornwall!'

Nev taps his speedo, as he has done every morning since it 'died', and we are excited to find that it is resurrected. Two days to go and we will again be able to 'clock' the speed and the distance.

Surrounded by lush pastures, the small Cornish towns were built, in ancient times, for the security and vantage of hill-tops. The 'lead' into villages usually involves conquering a sharp climb, followed by a squeeze into narrow cobbled lanes, now only one-way to safely direct the traffic flow. Buildings of stone and whitewash lean towards each other and hug closely together.

We follow miles of undulating terrain through the pretty countryside. Each climb, is for me, at a tempo dictated by someone else; but at least at a cadence that I am now thoroughly familiar with. The pattern of climb, drop, climb, is repeated all morning and this time we are heading directly into strong south-westerly winds, which are the usual reason why cyclists do 'LEJOG' (Lands End - John O'Groats).

The rain is literally 'bucketing-down', out of the sky, and we feel the need to dismount and get away from the deluge of stabbing wet needles. Cover is sparse, as has been the case almost every time on this trip that the rain has been at it's most earnest. Our choice of shelter, hugging the high bank, under a spindly tree, does little to provide the protection we need.

A break in the rain gives a sufficient interlude to allow us to picnic, on warm Cornish pasties, whilst sitting on the fence, outside the small Post Office store from which we made the purchase, in Upton Cross. The local postmaster was happy to pass the time of day; and mentions that he enjoys cycling. Giving one of the ensuing gradients legendary proportions he warns that he had, on his road bike, only twice cycled the hill to Minion; so with a fully loaded tandem, we set off in trepidation.

The offending hill is truly steep, but we have this wonderful granny gear that we have begun to rely on, and we have double the determination to 'make it'.

In fact I vow that as I had not walked in Scotland, well, apart from Leadhills that is, there is no way I am going to be beaten by the hills in Cornwall and succumb to walking. The effort of the climb is enormous and the pace is so slow that my speedo keeps flicking from three miles per hour to zero, and back again. Nev encourages our commitment to continue cycling by breathlessly saying, "Take it easy, just pretend we are walking, no effort, and just keep the legs turning easily." And there we have it, another climb achieved!

I notice a rather unpleasant smell and after a few tentative sniffs, I realise that it is emanating from me. A couple of nights ago, my cycle clothes had not dried. The next morning, they had been stuffed into a plastic bag, so as not to dampen other items during that day's travel. Last night they had again been hung to dry completely, and now they are on my body. The putrid smell, of stagnant clothing, mingled with men's deodorant (a weight saving decision to bring only one to share) and trapped sweat, is wafting out the neck of my raincoat, threatening to asphyxiate me. Yuk!

The climb delivers us to the bleak and largely desolate landscape of Bodmin Moor. Prevailing winds mow the grass blades flat and part the long shaggy wool of the black-faced sheep, as if with a comb. My fluorescent jacket is inflated with air, so my body resembles a bright yellow Michelin man.

Our route takes us on a narrow sealed road the ten miles across the Moor and, all the while, we battle directly into the wind. There are historic granite Tors in this region; mounds of granite that appear to have been stacked by ancient beings, but are actually layers of rock that have been exposed over hundreds of years, through the weathering by wind and water. These 'towers' dot the landscape of pasture, bracken and marshes.

Even our gradual descents through the towns of East Taphouse, Middle Taphouse, West Taphouse, Lostwithiel and Tywardreath and finally St Austell, near sea-level, are slowed by the wind we are facing head-on.

The shorter distance today means we arrive in St Austell about 4 p.m. This is going to be an early finishing day for us, but not as early as I would have liked. I had really wanted to visit the 'Eden Project' and it is for this reason that we chose St Austell as our destination for the night. It would be only six miles to the gardens. Alas, we really should have set off this morning at 6 a.m., if I really wanted to factor the visit into a cycling day. The last entry time to this horticultural spectacle is at 4.30, too late today, and we do not have time to visit tomorrow.

The Information Centre on the main road is a logical stopping point to get directions to the Stationhouse Bed and Breakfast, which we know is a little out of town. Also Penzance, our destination tomorrow, is to be the final night on this epic and is the only town where we had been unable to book accommodation on-line, while in Adelaide. The tourist officer suggests that we go to the supermarket, 200 meters away, and while we replenish supplies he will use the time to find accommodation in Penzance that suits our budget and which will secure a bike.

Having experienced dismal wintery conditions over the past few days, it seems so peculiar to see buckets and spades and beach paraphernalia displayed in the supermarket. I have completely forgotten that this is summer in England, and that we are in fact on the coast.

Our return to the Information Centre is well timed. We have only just stepped inside when the heavens open again. The tourist advisor had travelled parts of Europe on tandem tours with his wife, and is keen to talk about his experiences. We enjoy his hospitality of tea and biscuits, while we wait for the torrential downpour to subside. Thirty minutes later the deluge has finally reduced to a heavy drizzle. While conditions are still not ideal it is time we set off.

Having stopped at the supermarket and then being further delayed due to the weather conditions; we are no longer going to be settled in early for the evening. As has become almost the predictable ending to every day, we make our way, mostly uphill, three more miles to our destination, the Stationhouse Bed & Breakfast.

Day Fifteen Stats:

Distance covered: 57.86 kilometres, 36 miles (much less than the mileage we achieved in a day in Scotland)

Average speed: 10.7 kph (half the average we were achieving in Scotland)

Riding time: 5 hours 23 minutes (longer ride time than double the distance in Scotland)

Estimated Trip Miles total: 838.63

St Austell - Lands End - Penzance

Day Sixteen: UK
Thursday, 21st June

I hadn't been able to settle to sleep until the last train had passed at 11.30 p.m. It is the nature of station houses that they are adjunct a railway line, and this accommodation lives up to its name. The night had also been interrupted by the unexpected buzz of a door bell, seemingly at regular intervals. I was a guest here so didn't think too much about that sound, apart from that it seemed unusual. I was woken by the same buzzing well before the first morning train that rattled by at 6.50 a.m.

While we are eating breakfast the landlady asks, in a soft rather embarrassed inflection, "Did you hear the doorbell in the night?" then proceeds to explain that last night, the regular lodger had gone out for the evening. Our hosts hadn't realised this and he had been inadvertently locked out by them. They had not heard the doorbell, so he had slept in his car in the front yard.

I had woken with heaviness in the pit of my stomach. I should feel excited! This is going to be our last day of cycling in the UK. The despondency heaves into anticlimax. While getting to this point has been one hell of an achievement, I don't feel any the better for it. I don't even feel that it has been an admirable thing to do. Even within the circle of mountain bikers who we call friends, I don't know of anyone who would be envious of this achievement. It just isn't on anyone else's 'to do' list. In fact it seems quite pointless and selfish to have just done it for ourselves. I wish that we'd had the foresight, and 'lead-in time', to do this trip as a sponsored ride, so that some unfortunate child could have benefited in some way.

The final launch; from 'The Stationhouse', St Austell

Breakfast is taken in the conservatory room; a modern addition along the side of the house. Three walls are of glass to attract the sun's warmth; this morning they are frosted with the moist air, and I stare out, from my seat at the breakfast table, through the misty condensation at the abysmal weather. Squally rain is blowing horizontally across the fields. The last thing I want to do is put on the wet weather gear to spend another day outdoors in this terrible weather.

Our hosts, Mr and Mrs Warrander, watch as we saddle up. They wave, expressing good cheer. My emotions are close to the surface and I fight back tears as we negotiate the irregular surface of their gravel driveway. This journey has been my Everest. Not so much about attaining the summit, but the comparison is about committing to a challenging goal. Whole-hearted determination in taking on each day, and then achieving another after that, until we are now at the point where - in the words of Sir Edmund Hilary - it is time "to knock the bastard off"

Our guide notes are directing us towards Mousehole, a small village on the coast, and then continuing on minor roads through Lamorna to Lands End. The route is shown as a line on the map page that is so faint, it is almost invisible. The thread-like marking defines an arc-shape, near the coastal edge of England's south-western peninsular. This light coloured representation screams at me loudly of lanes and hills; quite possibly winding through stunning scenery, that will be washed out by the weather.

In our desperation to finish, we break our vow, made only three days ago, to avoid motorways, and decide to take the route of least resistance, the A30, the most direct route to Penzance. It would have been ideal if this route headed directly west, but first we must ride seven miles north, over undulating terrain to join the motorway.

I can't believe it! This is our final day cycling in Britain and my speedo has decided to work again.

The narrow shoulder on the edge of the two lane motorway gives insignificant spatial security. We have joined the main highway between Exeter and Penzance. There is a constant stream of cars and Lorries speeding by with little regard for our inconsequential mode of transport. I had imagined the conclusion to this adventure would be a sun-filled ride along coastal lanes, accompanied by the symphony of birds twittering in the English countryside. The wet conditions orchestrate only the relentless swish of tires.

The hills are monotonous. The reality of the height of the hills comes home to me, when I look to my right and find we are parallel with the blades of a wind farm, whipped into frantic oscillation by the gusts that we are riding head-on into. I look down at the tarmac, watch the drips fall repetitively from my helmet to splat the drink bottle cage, then splash to the road. Glancing up occasionally, I squint past Nev's wind inflated raincoat and flapping hood, only to see another 'rise' directly ahead. I've got it lucky! I am thankful that Nev is captaining this frigate. His shoulders are squared stiffly as he launches into battle directly into the wind. The rain is constant. Nev grips the handlebars in preservation mode, to keep us from being blown into the traffic. We cover the ground quickly enough, driven by fear rather than fitness.

Three cyclists, with their heads down in concentration, pass. Nev groans with the humiliation of being defeated, in what must now have, in his mind, become a race. After all there are now a number of cycles on the same road. I'm sure he would perceive it to be a tragedy to be passed, therefore 'pipped-at-the-post', so close to the finish line. The space created by their passing manoeuvre is helpful, as the traffic slows having now been confronted with the prospect of knocking over at least one of these four single-file skittles. We hug their tail, to ride slip-streaming, in relative ease for a brief time, before the distance, between us and these svelte weightless 'roadies', proves that any competition is to their advantage.

Ah! Our chance to take the lead is presented when the cyclists stop ahead at a roadside parking bay. Nev recognizes that the riders are the same group that we met outside the pub at Orton. We stop and accept their offer of a juice drink each. It is delicious and I wonder why I have never thought to buy such refreshment over the past few days. It is far superior in flavour to the one shared energy drink to which we treated ourselves every afternoon. The cyclists are a group of sixteen sponsored riders, also on the final leg of their pilgrimage. I am envious with thoughts of the camaraderie and efficiency of riding in a group, the hot lunches and evenings resting in pubs. The support van that travels slightly ahead of the group, with ready supplies of food and drink and comfort for those too tired to continue, is a luxury that I can only dream of. We share conversation of mutual experiences which, combined with the easing of the rain showers, lifts my spirits so that I feel in a much more positive frame of mind as we remount to continue.

The Golden Arches signifies for us a poor standard in cuisine, but an international standard in usually clean toilet facilities. Ablutions are the only reason we have entered a McDonalds on this trip and right now nature is calling for us to stop. Today though, the poster displaying the coffee and donut special is a tempting combination, so we succumb to making a purchase here, with the excuse that we need the sustenance to fortify us to complete our mission! With bodies wired from the caffeine and sugar hit, we easily travel the remaining ten miles to Penzance.

All of our bags are dropped at The Tremont B&B but our wet weather gear is kept handy for the last leg; nine miles to Lands End. With no load the bike is as frisky as a new born colt. We ride in good spirits, the rain has stopped and we have no doubt that with only fifty minutes to achieve our goal we are going to 'knock it off'.

The Lands End experience is quite different to the isolation of our start at John O'Groats. The greater number of visitors to this more populated end of the country means that the tourist industry is out for every buck that can be gleaned from travellers. The variety of bars, restaurants, tourist shops and exhibitions creates an almost carnival atmosphere. We don't have the heart to return to John O'Groats from Lands End, travelling by virtual experience. Posters explain the distance would be covered in a twenty minute viewing, at speeds of 6000 mph. We agree that this would trivialise the effort of the past sixteen days, so decide to bypass that form of entertainment. We get the final stamp to the CTC form, which is now a rather tatty piece of paper.

The photograph taken at Lands End records my blog title 'It Takes Two to Tandem' on the signpost overhead, and we are side by side, touching gently at the shoulders, Nev's hand resting over mine. The Team has made it!

I'm keen to share my achievement and phone home. "Hi Love, we have made it."

"Made What?" A dazed Chelsea responds.

"Dad and I have finished our UK tandem ride, and I am so happy I thought I'd let you know that we've finished, we made it and we're both alive."

"Mum? Do you realize that it is three in the morning? Do you want me to wake Levi and tell him?"

"No. Sorry to wake you. Go back to sleep and we'll talk again in a few days."

The 'End to End' journey's completion has gone to Nev's head. Drugged with euphoria he rides in mad mountain bike racing mode, the nine miles back to Penzance. I am convinced he does not want to be overtaken by any vehicle. With a tail wind at last, we scream down hills and around corners on the slick, wet road. The experience is simultaneously as frightening as it is exhilarating.

"Whoa!" I call. "Slow down! We're going forty miles an hour. I don't want to end up plastered on the tarmac!'

At times like this I would like to be in control of my own destiny and one pact I have made with myself, while travelling through the UK, is that from now on I will be.

Day Sixteen Stats:

Distance covered: 105 kilometres, 66.52 miles

Average speed: 20.3 kph

Riding time: 5 hours 15 minutes

'Team George' has made it!

Trip Miles total: 905.15

Penzance – Worthing

B oarding the train at Penzance is without mishap, even though the tandem is not boxed and is exposed. We haven't had any access to bike cartons or the necessary duct tape to disguise the beast for this train journey. When we get to Worthing, preparations for the next stage of our travel, to Europe by train, will be easily managed with help from our friends.

Opportunities to relax over the past days have been minimal, so it is pleasurable to sit in quiet companionship as we travel on the train towards London. I peer intently from the train window as we near St Austell, to catch a fleeting glimpse of the Stationhouse Bed and Breakfast that we had stayed at, during what seems like a long-distant, two nights ago. The speed of the train trivialises our physical efforts since then, as it blurs the accommodation and rushes us along the coastline through the lush countryside, to Plymouth and beyond.

"You know, it's odd; but I can't remember much of the past sixteen days. It's already blurring into a vague memory," Nev comments.

"Yeah," I agree, "it's the same for me." In reality though, for me it has been similar to my experience of childbirth. Once over, some aspects replayed in my head, tapping away repeatedly at the brain cells, until deeply embedded; other phases wafted off as if in a wispy haze, within seconds of the experience. There are moments on this trip that I will choose to forget, and others that will bring a flood of recollections that enable me to visualise even the most minuscule detail. Minutiae appear to have been tattooed on my brain, so that I will wear the experience forever.

We are worried about the short time-frame between disembarking from this London bound train and transferring at Reading to the train heading south to Worthing. With only ten minutes to complete the transfer, we are at the doors prepared to rush. The train jerks to a halt, doors have only half opened and we are already heaving our gear onto the platform. A cursory glance identifies there is a lift to our right. We are in the elevator, the bags are in, but the tandem will not fit even on an angle. Nev wheels the tandem into a sprint and rushes off, calling back to me over his shoulder "You take the bags and I'll meet you on the platform."

I am alone in the lift, pushing the button, but the lift does not appear to move. The doors open and I step out. No change to my surroundings confirms that I have not gone anywhere. A young lady gets into the lift and I call to her, "I don't think it is working!" Her response is enough of a quizzical expression, that I doubt my ability as a lift operator. I re-enter the lift and stand beside her. She presses the button and the lift rises. How stupid I have been; jabbing at the down button, expecting to have to go to the other platform by subway, instead of noticing that I have to cross by overbridge. As the lift doors open, I snatch up all of our bags and run across to the lift on the opposite side. This time, the button takes me down successfully.

I am beginning to feel panicked. I am afraid that Nev will catch the train and I will be stranded. Fear resonates in my head as the words, *'don't go without me, hurry, hurry, you can't miss the train; please still be there',* bounce around in my brain, forcing my legs to sprint, and encouraging me to ignore that my back feels broken and my arms stretched to tendon snapping capacity. My heart threatens to thump through my ribcage, as it pounds with exertion and apprehension. I am so worried that Nev will be on that train and I will miss it. I rush onto the platform to find Nev standing there, alone, beside the vacant line.

"Where the hell have you been?" he demands crossly. Then as his mouth stretches to a grin, follows the question with; "At least I touched it that time." This is just the acknowledgement I need to confirm that he had not been fast enough to board either.

The station master approaches and asks us where we are heading. He instructs us to wait. He won't allow us to take the next connection to Worthing, as we would then be into the time of peak traffic leaving London. Our fare is for 'off-peak' travel, and with the train crowded with commuters, we will not be able to get the bike on. We have no choice but to wait two hours, until the traffic will be lighter and our tickets validated. I phone my friend to let her know that we have been delayed.

Arriving much later in Worthing, the sun has already set and we are just in time to join the last moments of the barbeque that Sue has invited friends to; in honour of the completion of the British stage of our journey!

Part Two

PROVENCE & TUSCANY

London – Paris

Our plans include travelling on the Eurostar train from London to Paris. Train travel, or more precisely the catching of a train, to date hasn't been a positive experience, but this is the first time we have run into difficulties getting a ticket. Research undertaken prior to leaving home had given us an idea of what to expect the cost to be; we were also aware that to get the best deal, we needed to buy tickets at least seven days before our intended date of travel. While cycling in Cornwall we were too fixated on finishing the journey and getting out of the rain, and hadn't come across, or made the effort to find, an internet café to make the purchasing of tickets possible. We later found, when we were in Surrey with access to our friend's computer; we had left it too late. With only four days to departure, discount tickets were no longer available and the ticket office quoted £300 each. For a one-way ticket, that cost was ludicrous!

Through much Internet searching, Nev eventually located a travel agent, who for £150 each, secured two return tickets that included two nights in two-star accommodation in Paris. We intend using the tickets for one-way travel to Paris. The return ticket is not needed so will be thrown away. We will be staying only one night in the hotel. Having already booked and paid for two nights in a Youth Hostel, we have now doubled up on accommodation and will have to forfeit the first Youth Hostel night.

London; time for sightseeing but we still can't get away from the bike theme and daggy clothes.

The bike being oversized cannot travel with us on the Eurostar, so we have to deliver it to Kings Cross station the evening before our own departure date. We have been told that we will be expected to collect the tandem from the Gare du Nord station in Paris, probably the day after our arrival. Nev trundles the bike to the oversize luggage office, and is told, on checking it in, that the tandem will in fact be on the same train as us, so we can collect 'our baby' on arrival in Paris. Rather than being convenient, this is in fact unfortunate news. I feel like a parent who has been promised a night out and then the baby-sitter fails to show.

Not to worry, that is for tomorrow. At least tonight I will be able to forget about the tribulations of combining cycle touring with train travel. This is the second of the two nights we have designated to stay in London. Entertainment and relaxation is what we have planned. Visits to the theatre are at least forcing us to be seated for a while, as during the past two days, we have been walking miles around London revisiting areas we enjoyed when we lived here many years ago. Tonight we have tickets for the stage show 'Wicked'.

Last night we sat in 'the gods' and enjoyed the 'Lord of the Rings' stage show that has been open for only a couple of weeks. The show had been well received in Toronto, Canada, where it had opened last year but many London reviews had not been favourable. We were curious to see how JRR Tolkien's fantasy, that had taken New Zealander, Peter Jackson, ten years to bring to the big screen, could be condensed into a four hour stage production. At a cost of fourteen million pounds, it is possibly the world's most expensive theatre production and we reckon because of that, it may not get to Australia for years, if at all.

Forest creepers clung encroaching on the theatre walls and entwining the forward stalls to become the fragile stage at times. The finale of the first half was of the character Gandalf falling within the Mines of Moria. We were sitting 'up in the Gods' and the disappearance of Gandalf, lost to unknown depths was camouflaged by a fireball of eyebrow singeing heat intensity. An amazing spectacle!

Boarding the Eurostar from St Pancras Station is a fairly calm experience. We have luggage that is able to be carried easily between us, and have no cycle carriage to run for. We notice though, that Nev has not been allocated a seat. Installed in a fold-down dickie-seat beside the carriage doors, he has been advised to wait there until the train begins to roll. Fortunately there is no passenger beside me and he is later able to claim the unoccupied seat.

I wake in France. Having succumbed to the motion of the fast train, I fell into the deepest day-time nap I think I have ever had; my head didn't loll forward floppily on my neck, as is usually the case when I am in a travel stupor. I had no dreams and had even blocked out all sounds, so there were no interruptions to my reverie. I have entirely missed the vistas of southern England and the Chunnel which I had been looking forward to.

The pleasure of travelling unencumbered is worth maintaining for a little longer. On disembarkation we decide to leave our burden at the transport office overnight, as we had initially thought would be the case, rather than drag the tandem through the streets of Paris, just so that we could store it with us.

Morning in Paris, with us in holiday mode, should be delightful. We have however committed to travelling by, and with, the burden of the tandem, so firstly must take responsibility for it.

Our large panniers have been left at the hotel and we have just collected the boxed tandem from La Gare du Nord. Travelling with it by underground train, to the Youth Hostel in the suburb of Clichy, a few kilometres north of the city, is no easy matter. There are stairs to negotiate, and in the crowded carriage, we are embarrassed about how much space we are occupying. Nev tilts the carton ninety degrees to stand it on the narrow edge and we squeeze together to minimize our impact on those commuting.

Youth Hostels often have quirky rules and this one is no exception. It is mid-morning but we cannot check-in until 3.00 p.m. We are welcome to leave our gear, however another rule here is that all items of left luggage are to be stored securely and we are pointed in the direction of some lockers. We consider the luggage that is presently with us. The small panniers won't be an issue, they will fit easily. We are told the tandem is not exempt. This presents a problem, as it is quite obvious that there is not a locker large enough to contain it. Having arrived with the tandem, we do not want to leave again with it. Clearly we are not going to enjoy an afternoon in Paris with a boxed tandem in tow. After some discussion with the receptionist, we are permitted to leave the box and its contents in a room adjoining the office. With the storage of the major item of our luggage solved, we now need to secure the small panniers in a locker. Here is the third rule. Once shut, a one Euro coin has to be inserted to secure the locker. That seems sensible, but on turning to leave, we realise we have locked our wallet away. If we open the locker right now, it will cost another Euro to re-secure it. We don't want to pay another Euro just because of our stupidity, so discuss our predicament with the receptionist; to no avail. Rules are rules. We have already pushed the limits with our demands and there is no way we are going to be allowed to break another rule. Reluctantly the requisite coin is inserted.

Finally, but only for five hours, we have no luggage! The underground delivers us back to the city where, as is characteristic for us, we have a half day of our own self-guided tour. On foot, we skirt the exterior of the many historic places; admiring the elaborate architecture and by-passing the queues that snake towards the famous tourist sites, which we had explored thirty years ago. Savouring the experience of this historic city we amble slowly along the Seine and down the Champs-Elysees from L' Arc de Triomphe to the Louvre. It's a fast walk back from there to be at the hotel we stayed at last night, by four o'clock in the afternoon. Collecting our remaining luggage, we travel again the twenty minutes by underground, back to the Youth Hostel, check-in to our room, taking note of the bed set up; singles, of course, and head for separate bathrooms. Ten minutes later we are both showered and dressed in our finery; clothes that have been tucked away in the bottom of the panniers, just for this one evening.

A quick shake of my dress, made of crushed polyester, has restored it to a presentable state. My footwear is a pair of black, 'strappy' sandals that are virtually weightless. They are ten years old and unworn for at least the last five of those. After the evening, the shoes will have served the sole purpose for which they were brought along, and I will toss them in a bin!

Nev looks daggy and barely presentable in his navy hiking pants, that have zips mid-thigh for quick conversion to shorts. Beige Crocs on his feet are fortunately almost hidden by the trouser hem. What does it matter? It will be dark, his trousers and feet will mostly be tucked under a table and we don't know anyone here.

The night, recommended by a friend and pre-booked over the Internet long before we left Adelaide, is going to be an evening extravaganza. I am expecting a little taste of luxury that I have been excitedly anticipating. Our fourth underground trip today, takes us back to the inner city. From 6.00 p.m. to 1.30 a.m. we are to be in someone else's capable hands. As independent travellers on other journeys, we had derided the groups of tourists who huddled around guides identified by raised umbrellas. How pleasurable it is though, to sit on the coach. As passengers we travel calmly through the heavy traffic, without having to navigate unfamiliar routes, amongst vehicles that drive on, what for us would be, the wrong side of the road.

Our first scheduled stop is at the Eiffel Tower where we are privileged to follow the umbrella, held aloft by the guide, permitting us to jump the 200 meter long queue. I'm excited to be on the tower as when we visited back in '76 the weather was showery and, expecting to have a restricted view, we had decided not to part with the entrance fee. We had decided too, at that time, not to join the many other vans that had chosen the spot beneath the tower to be their free-camp-site, and had selected a more discreet camping spot, parked kerbside in a quiet street.

Taking the elevator to the first level, we are taken to the restaurant, to a dinner washed down with champagne. Following the meal, we choose to descend to ground level by the stairway option and are rewarded with a view of the sparkling lights of Paris. The umbrella then leads us to the riverside wharf and we board the boat for the Seine River Tour.

Back on land the umbrella guides us to another coach and we are driven to Moulin Rouge, for the 11.00 p.m. show. The seating and settling of patrons is a well-tuned affair, with people entering the theatre in groups that quickly fill the tiers. Beginning from front of stage, each party, once seated, is served sparkling champagne. The stewards confirm that everyone is settled and satisfied, then the staff move on, to serve the next section.

This Cabaret is spectacular, but half-way through I am almost overcome with exhaustion and maybe just a little intoxicated. It is not a feeling of sleepiness, but a deep weariness that spreads through my hips and back muscles making even the act of sitting, tiresome. My legs are aching and I feel like I really must lie down. Being horizontal is obviously not an option, but trying to stay relaxed yet alert is extremely difficult. I fidget and jiggle in my seat and make a resolute effort to remain focused.

The others in our tour group have the luxury of being delivered, after the show, back to their central city hotels. When we boarded the bus earlier in the evening, in response to "What Hotel are you staying at?" we replied that we were staying at the Youth Hostel at Clichy. We were told that the bus didn't go that far north, but not to worry, as Moulin Rouge was in that general direction, and it would be best for us to get a taxi afterwards. Fortunately we manage to hail a cab and make it known to the taxi driver the suburb we need. He drops us on a road at a point that looks familiar in the Clichy vicinity, leaving us with just a short walk to the hostel.

Later Nev tells me that while watching the cabaret tonight he has become aware that he needs spectacles. He had enjoyed the show and was aware that some of the acts were performed by topless women, but had disappointedly not been able to see much detail!

Paris – Avignon

In the wee small hours of the morning we arrive at the hostel to experience constantly interrupted sleep. Other guests return throughout the early morning and, as the room doors are made of steel, there is a resonant clanging that announces each new arrival. A sleep-in is also out of the question. As we have no idea what the future may hold, today will possibly be our last in a life-time opportunity to explore the city. We are due to leave Paris today; late afternoon.

Northern Europe is also suffering from the rain and cool temperatures we experienced in England, in fact Paris has also been quite cool and I have wandered the streets amongst the chic Parisians looking daggy in my Gore-Tex raincoat, to keep warm. Now it is time to head south, hopefully to warmer weather as, in contrast, the forecast indicates that Southern Europeans are suffering, and some are dying in the heat. We have a train booked for Avignon later in the day.

During the past two days, as we walked the streets of Paris, we have been fascinated by the number of very small vehicles, particularly 'Smart' cars that were sometimes huddled two together, to share one parking space. To make our departure from Paris easier, we need a taxi van, or similar vehicle, large enough to transport us, and our gear, to the station. Because of our very limited knowledge of the French language, yesterday we had explained our need for a taxi van to the receptionist at the Youth Hostel, and were reliant on him making the phone call on our behalf, to book the transport.

Unfortunately the receptionist has forgotten to make the phone call and indicates that now, at this time of the morning; he is too busy to help us. Having already experienced the awkwardness of travelling with all our gear on crowded underground trains, we decide it is best to begin preparing for our late afternoon departure from Gare du Lyon, using the same method as when we arrived; moving our luggage in relay.

Dressed in our finery for dinner at the Eiffel Tower

The first chore of the morning is to take all of our bags to Gare du Lyon, using the underground. This will be a precursor to the tandem run. That is, we will have knowledge of the route, specifically the underground platform transfers, as well as, and more importantly, how many stairs and escalators are to be negotiated on the trip. Carrying just the panniers and other smaller bags, and with the advantage of four arms between us, this is a smooth operation. Leaving the bags in the station baggage storage area, we are now able to make the most of the few hours we have left in the city.

The Latin Quarter usually teems with a bohemian vibrancy, but this morning Paris is having a 'sleep-in' and we have the narrow streets virtually to ourselves. Strolling leisurely through the Île de la Cité we arrive at Notre Dame, where we admire the impressive gargoyles and sculptures, before window shopping our return to the underground station.

Travelling back to the Youth Hostel mid-afternoon, another trip by underground, is for the specific purpose of collecting the tandem that we have kept boxed. We had no intention of cycling in Paris and thought the box would maintain a semblance of disguise, hopefully to avoid any possible issues on the next train journey that will transport us to Provence. The decision to make two separate trips today from the hostel to Gare du Lyon station was simply because it seemed the best way for us to cope with manhandling too much gear. For this leg of the underground journey we now only have the tandem.

Nev is suffering from tendonitis in his left arm, the inflammation caused by the constant strain of lifting and dragging our beast during the past couple of weeks.

On this short underground trip, much as I try to help, my assistance is negligible. Nev has cut handholds at each side of the front of the carton. Fortunately he is left-handed and I am right-handed, so we take our respective sides and perambulate the contraption, pulling it along secured to the little suitcase trolley. Because of the number of people about, this isn't as easy as it might seem, particularly on congested stairways. Nev is often too impatient to wait for me to assist, and I feel less than adequate, as too often I am chasing his back trying to keep up, instead of being helpful.

It is easier for me to give up. Instead of helping, I trail along behind, trying not to think too hard about my expectation of a fulfilling, albeit brief, experience of this vibrant city, that has in reality been more about hours spent relaying luggage and looking at the dark walls of underground tunnels.

At one point during this transition, Nev lifts the entire boxed bike, raising it over his head and higher than the heads of the surrounding throngs so that he can negotiate a crowded stairway. A young man smiles at me, raises his arm, bends his elbow and with biceps now flexed taunt, displays the international symbol of strength, while pointing to Nev's disappearing back. My response is a nod of agreement, followed by circling my fingers around my ears to indicate 'also just a little crazy!'

By the time we get to Gare du Nord station, for the second time today, Nev has lifted the thirty kilogram package up a number of flights of stairs. Exhausted, he plops himself down on the floor of the shopping arcade that defines the station perimeter.

"I'll wait here" he says, "you go and find the shortest route to the baggage room."

Leaving Nev I go in search of the baggage room. There is a wall about two hundred meters long, supporting the next level of a car park. Obviously people do not comply with the signage displayed on pillars that requests; 'do not urinate in this area' as it reeks of urine. I quicken my pace, wishing as I walk along, that I had stayed put. The ammonia smell is almost asphyxiating, besides Nev could have done the scouting. He has a much better sense of, and memory for direction.

I have no idea of the layout of the station and take a while to find the easiest way to get from the baggage room back to where Nev has planted himself. When I do finally make my way back, Nev is a little tetchy. I have been gone forty minutes and he had not expected me to be very long. Putting my orientation skills to the test, I am pleased to say that I easily guide Nev directly to the baggage room by a quick route.

My short-term memory has been working remarkably well whilst in Paris. I have been able to remember street names and underground routes and platform names. Having also, just now, successfully navigated the station, I have renewed confidence in my mental ability and trust that, having had six days off the bike; the full functioning of my brain is now restored.

With an hour until departure, we sit soaking up the sunshine, in a piazza outside the station, surrounded by all the paraphernalia required for our travel. Teenagers playing roller hockey on the vast smooth expanse of the piazza provide light entertainment. We sit beside two old men, topped in berets, whose unkempt appearance gives the impression of homelessness. Between them they are devouring a BBQ chicken. Nev wanders off and returns with a packet of four Magnums. Always looking for the best value, he found that, as in Australia, it is cheaper to buy a box of four ice-creams from the supermarket, rather than two single items from the deli. This gives us a treat, and the remaining two ice-creams are handed to our elderly neighbours for dessert, and received with thanks.

Still with thirty minutes until departure, we move into the large hall in full view of the departure board. "This is as nerve racking as waiting for the dentist," Nev's comment reflects my own anxious feelings.

On this train we are not expecting any problems. We have tickets, seats allocated, the bike is also booked, and we are actually early.

We board the train, stow the bike, fitting it snugly against the outside wall in the carriage's space allotted for bikes, and locate our seats. Sitting comfortably and feeling just a little smug, our respite is broken when a guardsman approaches wanting to know if the carton is ours. The guardsman's facial expressions and gesticulations make it clear there is a problem. Even with little knowledge of the language spoken, we get the general gist that all is not well. My poor translation establishes that he wants the bike hung up on hooks that are fitted in the luggage compartment for that purpose. Our bike is in a carton, a bit awkward to meet that requirement and it's just as difficult to get the guard to understand our English explanation, which is that we can see no problem with having the carton just how it is, where it is, out of the way in our opinion, and that we actually have no intention of complying with whatever demand he is making. The language barrier proves helpful. He gives up, moves on, and we breathe a sigh of relief but the brief altercation has left me feeling tense. Later in the journey the guardsman comes by, makes a laugh "Ha ha!" directed at us; then in a joke-like way rattles on about "la bicyclette" and various other words I do not understand. I feel like he is laughing at how he has been the instigator of my unease. I found no aspect of the situation humorous, and respond to his mirth with a cold stare.

Our arrival at Avignon is at 22:00. As we have no idea where the motel is situated, and as our large box will not be able to fit in a taxi, we phone the motel proprietor for directions. The suburb is only 1.2 km away; not too far if only a brisk walk was involved, yet too far to walk with all our gear. The proprietor kindly offers to pick us up in his van.

A very small van pulls up outside the station. Nev sits in the back holding the box that extends out the slightly ajar, rear double doors. Our driver tells us he is taking a less direct route. The direction is only slightly longer on minor roads as he wants to avoid meeting a policeman. It is illegal to drive with a passenger in the back.

Avignon – Gordes

Day One: Provence
Sunday, 1st July

Rays of soft sunshine reaching through the window, tickle my face into a gentle waking. The promise of a truly glorious day, that will be our first in three weeks, encourages us to get moving.

Nev is outside rebuilding the tandem and I am packing as scantily as possible. I'm feeling good; maybe even just a little excited as I prepare for our holiday in Provence. I very much want the sunshine to last, but optimism is not natural for me so I seek affirmation from the motel proprietor. When I ask if we should expect rain the response is that it is not the rainy season, so rain is unlikely. We have learned the importance of travelling light, so on this forecast, raincoats are stowed in the carton with other miscellaneous items. The carton, filled with items not required, is tucked in a corner of the motel laundry, for our collection when we return to Avignon on Friday.

Exploring Avignon, the heart of Provence, is the morning's priority. Having sung of it as children, in social studies classes, we know there is a bridge here. As adults we are learning of the historic importance of La Pont D'Avignon and the city it supported. Built during the 12th Century as the only southern crossing point of the Rhône River; it was later abandoned in the 17th Century. Today there remain only four of the original twenty-two arches and a Romanesque chapel dedicated to the bridge's patron saint.

Back in the 14th Century, Avignon became the capital of the Christian world with the arrival of the popes. The Palais Des Papes is the largest Gothic Palace in Europe. Of gigantic proportions, it was hardly a humble home for the Sovereign Pontiffs in the 14th Century.

Beside 'La Pont D'Avignon', France

We've almost worn ourselves out traipsing the cobbles in the heat but now its early afternoon and we need to leave Avignon. We haven't had lunch and can't understand why there are no shops open. Unable to get food supplies we decide to move on anyway.

Avignon - Gordes

Narrow cobbled streets are lined with colourful posters, advertising an arts festival, due to open later this week. Late last night we had noticed people out with bundles of posters and rolls of twine, industriously tying posters to every balustrade; and there were many. Along the edge of the lanes, bright spectacles of colour advertising theatre performances, now hang aloft, decorating almost every wrought iron balcony. It's easy to make our way through the peaceful maze of the old town, as the streets are devoid of vehicles and pedestrians. Navigation is straight-forward, as all the central streets radiate out to the ring-road that circulates the city just outside of what remains of the surrounding 14th Century ramparts.

From the Ring-Road, a right turn onto the aptly named Avenue de Folie (folly?), leads to our demise. We understand the avenue will take us to the very outskirts of the town, and then we will link to a country road that will lead us towards Gordes. A couple of kilometres along the avenue the tarmac 'peters-out'. We find ourselves in an empty shopping centre car park. There is no-one about so we ride footpaths and bump down kerbs until we have done a complete circuit of the shopping centre. Consulting the map gives no clue as to how we ended up here in the first place. The map is completely unhelpful in guiding us to a recognizable point as it's a tourist brochure and there is no defined detail of minor roads. I'm not convinced that just heading blindly in this direction will take us to a road that will be on the map. The compromise is to return to a point where we can get our bearings. Fortunately we don't have to back-track too far. Apparently we did not notice a veer in the road and had inadvertently changed direction at that point. Recovering our position we travel more confidently towards the outskirts of the city. When we eventually come across the country road with signage directing to Gordes, Nev suggests I could have relaxed a little and trusted his directional instincts.

Within five minutes we have a pretty view to our right of the Rhône River and Pont D'Avignon, with the walled city and the Palais des Papes beyond. The visual reward from this undulating vantage point also brings with it a painful reminder. Travelling in an uphill direction requires effort that transfers all too quickly, to stretched lungs and tired legs. I'm still whinging to myself about the hill effort, when I feel raindrops. Within moments the drops develop into miserable rain.

On our right, there is a tall solid fence that secures a grand mansion. Without raincoats we choose to pull over and sitting on the driveway, with backs leaning against the wall we are provided with a little shelter. While sitting and munching on fruit, I try desperately hard not to focus on the negativity of our current situation. After a six day reprieve we've been back on the bike for less than an hour and have experienced navigational uselessness, hills and precipitation. *'Hey this is France, the holiday of our journey, it's going to be great',* I try to reassure myself. Positive thoughts really can impact on the cosmos. Truly, those clouds moved aside. The break-through of warmth from the summer sunshine dispels my gloomy doubts.

It is mid-afternoon and having expended the energy to cover sixteen miles; our stomachs are long overdue for lunch when we arrive at I'sle sur la Sorgue. Food has been the topic of our conversation for the past half-an-hour and we head straight to the bakery, for the nourishment of those delectable French pastries that are internationally famous; Quiche Lorraine followed by baked Custard Flan.

Wandering lazily alongside canals, prettily bordered with café umbrellas and wrought iron fences supporting baskets of vibrant geraniums, our equilibrium is restored. The crisscross of waterways through the town lead us to remnants of the morning Flea Market; and the casual viewing of an array of handicrafts, interspersed with bright splashes of purple, gold and yellow displays of dried artichoke flower heads and ornamental gourds.

Virtually flat, with a smooth road surface, the five mile ride to Fontaine de Vaucluse is a cyclist's delight. Even though we are in Europe, where travel is measured in kilometres, as it also is in Australia and New Zealand; I am still referring to miles. Nev's cycle computer is not functioning again, and my speedo only records miles!

On the edge of the village, down by the river in the shade of an enormous oak tree, stacks of wooden boxes are piled beside stalls displaying fresh fruit. We are offered a sample and as a result of the ensuing taste sensation, pulpy orange sweetness, we purchase a kilo of the most delicious tree ripened apricots. While negotiating this purchase another vendor encourages us to sample his wine. A bottle of Rosé is purchased and stowed in the pannier. This is exactly how I dreamt a Provencal holiday would be.

We don't intend this trip to be the epic that England was. There is no Everest on this part of our journey. With shorter riding distances planned, I hope the effort will be more like that required to enjoy a cycling 'stroll' in foothills. Accommodation booked, more upmarket than Youth Hostels, sometimes for two consecutive nights, will allow us to explore scenic loops; gear free. I intend to have evenings enjoying good food, washed down with regional wines. I have lifted my self imposed alcohol ban, as without a strenuous 'next day', I will not have to worry about how my body is going to cope.

The pavement bordering the main street of Fontaine de Vaucluse is brightly decorated. Displays of embossed and patchwork quilts, interspersed with hanging, breeze wafted, wheat sheafed and sunflower decorated table cloths, are beautiful examples of local industry. These handcrafts would be very tempting for the average tourist, but having no room to carry anything other than our absolutely necessary gear, we can only admire. Beyond the stone buildings of the village, not too far distant, are the steep-sided canyon-like walls of a large mountain range.

"Don't worry Louise," Nev assures me, "we aren't going up there. Our accommodation is three kilometres out of Gordes."

Fortunately we are riding the flat roads of the valley floor. Gordes however remains clearly in sight and looms larger as we close the distance to the seemingly impenetrable hill it is atop. A large church or municipal type of building dominates the peak, surrounded by multi-level residences almost camouflaged, as they spill-down and cling to the same honey-gold coloured stone of the mountain.

We can't find on our map, the road where our accommodation is situated. The road doesn't have a name, only identified as D156. I ask a roadside fruiterer if he knows of it, but he doesn't. He does indicate that a three kilometre radius around the hilltop that Gordes balances upon, does actually cover quite a large area.

Our accommodation is also not a name he is familiar with.

Near the turn-off to Gordes there is a roadside information map. We both look at it intently but are unable to find the road. Nev goes back to the tandem and impatiently calls "Come on Lou, let's get going."

"Get going to where?" I reply "I'm not going up there!" My exclamation follows my finger pointing upwards towards Gordes. Turning my attention back to the map, I scour in a systematic 'Where's Wally' type of search. My determination is eventually rewarded. D156 is a right-hand turn off the road we are travelling on, just at the bottom of the hill to Gordes. Whew!

The road is located easily and we slow at every gate looking for our accommodation. We have cycled a couple of kilometres, and are now facing a T-intersection indicating we have travelled the entire length of D156, without finding any accommodation with the name 'd'almandier'. I have the phone number in the PDA so make a call. The lady at the other end of the line has heavily accented but understandable English, which is just as well, because my French is too limited to hold a telephone conversation. We establish that there is not a room for us tonight, they have no vacancy, but we are booked with them for tomorrow. The lady on the other end of the phone indicates that she may be able to help us find alternative accommodation nearby, but to take advantage of that offer I need to know where they are situated. She mentions words that I think sounds like "the farm", and then our call disconnects!

Just as we were preparing to leave home and double-checking our itinerary, we noticed that we had not confirmed a night's accommodation for July 1st.

We had booked July 2nd so hastily sent an email requesting the additional, previous night, but had not received a reply. It is now 7:00 p.m. July 1st. Our predicament is looking grim, as we have no-where to stay, we do not know where this place is that can help us. We know there is very limited accommodation in this area, and I am feeling really concerned that I may have to sleep in a ditch.

As I relay to Nev the snippets of conversation that I have understood, but that seem to me to have made our situation even more confusing, he remembers.

"I reckon 'd'almandier' was the name of the room that I booked; the place must be called something else."

On checking the email saved on the PDA we find the internet address lafermedelahuppe – the farm of something. Cycling back down the few kilometres of narrow road is now at a very slow pace, as we again scrutinise all the gate signs. Finally, just a few hundred meters from where we first entered the D156 road, the 17th Century old farmhouse is located. Later we learn that 'The Farm of the Huppe', is named for the Huppe, a migratory bird of the region. The nests of the bird were found in the fields when additional accommodation was built.

The receptionist was genuine with her offer of help and she phones the Auberge, - a lodge nearby - but they have no room. There is another place she can try for us but first she asks "Are you very tired?" We tell her that today has been quite easy for us and we are not too tired. She telephones La Mas de Belle Combe. "Yes," she nods towards us, "they have a room."

The price is, for us, an extremely steep 140 EU for the night and the location is at the top of an extremely steep hill, within the village of Gordes. We have no option but to go there and I wonder if we are ever going to be able to get to a night's accommodation, while we are on a cycling stage of this trip, without having to arrive in a state of total exhaustion. We look up at Gordes, sitting at a height of 635 metres, at the top of a virtually vertical cliff.

"Okay, it's a huge challenge so let's take it on!" Actually the discussion is rather one sided as Nev decides that we will be able to climb this gradient. Although I don't find his enthusiasm convincing I feel obligated to take my seat on the rear and follow. Straight away, Nev drops the gears all the way down to 'granny' and we climb doggedly, at not much faster than walking pace. In reality I am just as resolute as Nev, also wanting to achieve the summit without stopping. I don't care that my pedalling technique has reverted to pushing rather than rotating, or that my chest is as taut as a drum. I concentrate on just keeping my legs turning and rather than focusing on my rasping breaths, force myself to enjoy the stunning view of the valley floor that is slowly dropping away.

Nev and I are frugal travellers and at equivalent to $224 Australian, La Mas de Belle Combe is the most expensive accommodation we have ever stayed in, through our entire married life. The rustically beautiful room features a king-size bed, headboard pressed against a stone wall. One wall is whitewashed and has the small window set deeply; an indication of the wall's thickness. The furniture includes a hand painted wardrobe in the Provencal style; panels of twittering birds adorn the background that is a little crazed to create the illusion of antiquity. Each panel is framed in floral borders of cerise. The plaster ceiling is supported by enormous exposed wooden beams. There is a huge separate bathroom with bath. Sample size L'Occitane toiletries for our use, are displayed invitingly. On opening the double wooden-shuttered doors my gaze skims over the stone path and above the purple haze of blooming lavender, towards the mist shrouded outline of Le Petite Luberon mountain range across the valley.

The panniers are thrown in a corner. Our climbing is not yet complete for the day. We may not have stairs to climb to our room at this accommodation, as our room is at the same level as the gravel car park, but we have worked up an appetite and the town centre that is skirted by restaurants catering to tourists is ten minutes walk away, further uphill.

Distance covered: 37.39 miles.

Average speed: 10.4 mph.

Riding time: 3 hours 33 minutes

Gordes – Gordes

Day Two: Provence
Monday, 2nd July 2007

Rain pours down during the night. I lie in bed, on the brink of tears, thinking that the first thing we will need to do in the morning is go back to Avignon to get our raincoats. On waking, although the ground is still glistening wet, the sky is a cloudless azure. Unfortunately it isn't pleasant enough to breakfast outside on the verandah with the stunning valley view spread out before us.

Breakfast is presided over by our host Alain, who had retired to this new establishment from an occupation that culminated in the engineering of machinery that makes the twists of wire securing champagne corks to bottles. The meal is simple fare of bread, croissants, a selection of sweet, fruity home-made jams washed down with coffee. Alain explains that it is difficult to identify the old from the new in this region, as strict building codes ensure that any new facade is in keeping with historic buildings. He explains that there is a modern roof and guttering hidden beneath the exterior clay tiles that we see.

We check-out of the room but leave all our gear, except for the lunch bag. Setting off for a day of what we expect should be easy exploring, as we will be riding a virtually weightless tandem and are already perched on the highest point in the area. The little medieval town of Gordes, promoted as one of the most beautiful villages in France, is a delightful picturesque presentation of unspoiled, ancient stone houses that hug the slopes, and are linked by narrow cobbled streets.

At a casual cruising pace, we travel through the stunning rural landscape. The countryside is beautiful, with valley walls blanketed richly with shrubbery. Shades of green descend to meld into the purple hues of blooming lavenders that densely blanket the valley floor. The road is narrow and the space a little tight at times, as we share the tarmac with tourist traffic slowly snaking around the twists and turns as it makes its way in the same direction. We relax into a long steady climb that allows us to maintain a comfortable pace, followed by the enjoyment of an even longer steady downhill into the lavender-filled isolated canyon in which nestles the Abbaye de Sénanque.

The abbey is a huge stone structure that, from a distance, gives the appearance of a solid barn or fortress, except there is a softer circular aspect resembling a baptistery with church-like bell tower topped with a tiny cross. Loitering around the bookshop full of religious texts, we are disappointed to note we will have to forgo the Abbey tour, as it is not until 14:30. With other sight-seeing plans today, we are unable to stay that late into the afternoon.

Steady 'climbing' takes us the three kilometres up and out of the valley. A roadside rocky outcrop makes an ideal spot to recover from the climb and a comfortable seat on which to enjoy the view whilst lunching on the last of the apricots. Continuing our circular route we loop back to Gordes to collect the panniers.

It is now time to venture off this precipice. The downhill ride to the valley floor is a, jamb-myself-on-the-seat, grip-the-handlebars and brace-against-the-pedals, kind of descent. Extremely steep, it is not enjoyable, but very quickly delivers us to Ferme de la Huppe, where we drop our gear and venture off, unencumbered again, for the afternoon. Our first stop is to be a visit to a nearby Lavender museum. The route takes us through St-Pantaléon, a sleepy little village where there is no vehicle or person in sight, and no shops open.

We realise that we have forgotten about the European tradition of taking a siesta early in the afternoon. Our navigational difficulties are haunting us again, as we are unable to find the road that will take us to the lavender museum. The temperature is a stifling twenty-six degrees, which feels much more intense, out and exposed on the dark road surface. Suddenly, visiting a lavender museum is not something that I feel I really must do, and chances are it will be closed at this time anyway due to the siesta. Abandoning the visit, we ride on to Goult, another village that is in a comatose state. Following the base of the Petit Luberon, on the western side of the Luberon mountain range, we climb to, and pass through Ménerbes, which is also consistent with the other villages of the region, clinging to the hilltop. The scenery from here is stunning. The valley is laid out in a patchwork of small farms of grain, lavender and vine. On the opposite side of the valley, Gordes, where we started from today, hugs the edge of the Plateau de Vaucluse cliffs. To the right, the shining bald-headed peak of Mont Ventoux is visible.

I had nightmares about coming to this region, so close to that peak; often a hill climb feature of the Tour de France. If Nev decides he is going to do something, he is fully committed and never gives up. In my dreams Nev would insist that we 'summit' the Mont, so that we can experience the downhill switchbacks we have seen on television. He would badger me to tandem it with him. I usually try not to disappoint him but in my dream I become resolute in my determination not to even try. It is not the climb that concerns me. My worry is about gaining too much speed, zigzagging haphazardly, like a quickly deflating balloon, and trying to keep traction around the tight switch-backs, with those fearfully steep drop-offs. Nev ignores what he considers is my pathetic refusal, and goes it alone, riding like a madman, solo, on a tandem that is soon out of control. As usually happens in dreams, at this point I would wake in panic, never to witness the consequences, which I assume would be disastrous. Fortunately some dreams do not come true, and we now continue together sedately riding the tandem to the village of Oppède-le-vieux.

Restoration of this little historic village has been undertaken by the artists and writers who have taken up residence here. Climbing up the steep trail in the heat, I can only admire those who have carried up their tools and materials and been diligently working on the restoration of the Notre Dame d'Alydon church, built in the 13th Century.

Early evening we conquer the last steep climb of the day, to arrive at Lacoste which is to be our dinner destination. There are a number of restaurants on the main road with stunning views out over the valley towards Grand Luberon and Plateau du Parc, from which we started our day's ride. Instead of eating at one of these restaurants, with menu prices escalated as if we also must pay for the view, we select a small establishment away from the main route. Settling at one of only three tables set el fresco, on the edge of the narrow cobbled street; we choose the menu du jour. Entrée of salad, main of Chicken Provencale, served with pasta, is followed by Fromage Chevre (goat's cheese) decorated with aromatic Basilie (tiny Basil leaves). The finale is a dessert tart of custard and apple. My stomach is ready to burst!

Back on the tandem, the first two and a half miles are such a wonderful downhill gradient, that we do not have to pedal at all. Just as well we can be lazy; it will give the meal a chance to settle. Still with effortless bliss, we continue another eight miles enjoying the balmy evening, chasing the failing light; arriving back at our room 'd'almandier', on the darker side of dusk. We finish the evening with a cooling swim in the pool; 'stroking' the water discreetly so as not to disturb other guests who are enjoying an el fresco meal on the adjoining terrace. The restaurant here is very popular, bookings are essential and the proprietors expressed surprise when we said we would not be eating at their establishment. I'm sure the meal, which exceeds the tight travel budget we set ourselves, is well worth the cost of 45 Eu ($72 Australian) per person.

Distance covered: 42.90 miles.

Average speed: 11.4 mph.

Riding time: 3 hours 45 minutes

Gordes – Apt

Day Three: Provence
Tuesday, 3rd July 2007

The terrace is a beautiful venue for our breakfast of bread, croissants and jam washed down with coffee served in a large bowl instead of a mug that we are familiar with. Another 'blue sky morning' heralds anticipation of a really good day on the tandem. It is not just the beautiful weather that elevates our mood. We have decided that the distance of about sixty kilometres, that we are now covering each day, is the ideal distance for a tandem holiday. We are not exhausted, there is no need to hurry to get out of bed, there is time to explore, taking in the sites while travelling, and we have time to relax in the evenings, enjoying a bottle of local wine between us.

Again, fully loaded, we set off, heading for Apt, which will be our destination for the next two nights. The first part of our travel today, is an easy cycle along the flat valley floor. In the distance a huge harvester is travelling toward us. Keeping an eye on its progress, as the road seems too narrow to share; we consider 'evacuation' options. As expected the vehicle is too broad and size takes precedence! To avoid getting caught in the machinery, we leap off quickly, hauling the tandem with us, into a shallow ditch at the side of the road.

We spend the morning, on foot, exploring the streets of Roussillon. We have learned now that the locals take their siesta seriously; this is the reason why, on other days, we have gone hungry in the early afternoon, unable to find food. The bakery is open, so we purchase supplies for lunch. Baguette, Chevre and tomatoes, form the basis of the gourmet picnic that we consume in the shade of a tree in the village centre.

Yesterday we had discussed the likelihood of our teenage children enjoying travel to the rural regions of France, and had decided; probably not! Today our lunch-time companions are a Canadian tourist, who is travelling with her two teenagers. They tell us that, while their mother is soaking up the history and architecture of these historic villages, they are not really enjoying the area at all. They speak animatedly of enjoying the shopping, internet cafes and the grand historic sites of Paris, but rural France holds no excitement for them.

These villages are not as technologically advanced as small towns in rural Australia. We haven't seen the internet for days, some villages do not have an ATM, and most shops and restaurants do not take credit cards. The village shops consist mostly of one of each of La Poste, Patisserie-Boulangerie, Fruiterer-Grocery, at least one shop selling tourist wares and maybe two Restaurants that I expect are for the tourist, rather than local trade. People wandering at mid-day are tourists; locals have disappeared into their homes for siesta induced invigoration. Everything closes from 12:00 until 15:00; a break that ensures the locals only work their thirty-five hours per week, as shops remain open until late into the evening. We have now learned to buy our food early in the day, as it is too difficult to continue biking until late afternoon, on only the calories gained at breakfast (and I am sure they are many, especially when two croissants are consumed).

Looking relaxed in Gordes, France

     Away from the stone and cobbles of the medieval architecture, much of this area, having similar smells and humidity, reminds me of the Asian villages we have travelled through on other journeys. There is none of the window dressing we are familiar with at home. Shop fronts are usually closed and secure, with a roller-garage type of door, streets are narrow, bordered by houses of plaster and tile. Public toilets are often 'starting blocks', which I usually prefer in terms of comfortable expulsion; however my legs are so tired, that when I squat to use them, I have to brace myself by jamming my elbows into the wall either side, to reduce the screaming in my thighs, and so as not to fall-over.

Riding this morning has been a mixture of the joy and ease of smooth flat roads, punctuated by the exertion of the short sharp climbs through the villages. Summer daylight hours are long, and this sunny afternoon we decide to take all the daylight hours we need to enjoy the journey. The chosen route is a scenic loop to Apt, stopping at each of the charming villages of St Saturmin, Les Apt and Rustrel. Situated at the foot of Mont De Vaucluse, these villages are, as has been typical of villages in this region, each sprawled over the rise of a single steep hill.

Just beyond Rustrel is the National Park, Colorado Provencal, which we visit. On foot, we explore this area of ochre cliffs and 'buttes', a vivid contrast to the rich green of the forested mountains. Ochre, and the making of paints has been a major industrial product of this region, and the houses look resplendent in their display of blue shuttered windows, being the only bright contrast to the many hues of the rusty colour of ochre.

The final leg of our ride today, is a delightful downhill 'cruise', through vineyards and lavender fields which delicately perfume the air. I am so thankful to have the experience of travel to this region. I am also extremely proud of my old legs, for having brought me this far.

Distance covered: 30.69 miles.

Average speed: 11.1 mph.

Riding time: 2 hours 44 minutes

Apt

Day Four: Provence
Wednesday, 4th July

The first of two nights we are to spend at Auberge du Luberon in Apt, allows us to catch up with washing; alas some chores still need to be done! The bath is filled, and after a quick wash of ourselves, we throw our entire wardrobe in, apart from what we are wearing, to soak while we set off to a supermarket. Provisions for tomorrow; samples of some of the regions produce, including sweet fruit confits, wine, and beers, fill our basket. Another bottle is slipped in; Pastis - an aniseed aperitif - that I want to try, having read about it in Peter Mayle's book 'A Year in Provence'.

Neither of us has any idea how we should drink the local liquor. It seems sensible to take the Pastis straight, like a liqueur. While our simple pasta meal is cooking on the 'Pocket Rocket' stove that is balanced on the tiny, street-facing, window-sill balcony, the Pastis, that tentatively touches the lips, is sampled with sips. The process of drinking is as slow as if we are administering a nasty medicine!

Next morning is easily whittled away, poking around in the art and tourist shops. With a population of 11,000, Apt is a small town, well known for its candied fruits (fruit-confits) that are displayed artistically in shop windows, amongst the delectable towers of rich chocolate. The old town of narrow cobbled streets, winding between houses, provides nooks and crannies to explore.

A rare visit to a cycle shop needs to be scheduled. Nev appears to me to be rather over protective of the tandem, as he explains in depth to the cycle mechanic what he considers to be the problem. Finally having quizzed the mechanic enough to be satisfied that he is in fact competent, we leave him to adjust the drive chain, the only repair needed in all these days of touring.

Tonight we brave another session of Pastis. There is still half the small bottle to drink and we are not good at wasting produce, even when the choice is not a good one. Nev discovered today that Pastis is to be taken with water; however the additional volume does little to improve the taste, but rather further prolongs the agony. We persevere with a few more sips, before eventually flushing the remaining liquid down the toilet.

Apt – Pernes-Les-Fontaines

Day Five; Provence
Thursday, 5th July

As we are to leave France tomorrow, travelling by train to Italy, today we need to start closing 'the loop' that we are riding; taking a 'line' back towards Avignon. Although we are thoroughly enjoying our visit to Provence, we feel limited by our mode of transport, as the distances we are able to cycle are small, giving just a taste of what the region can really offer. Tempted, but unable to experience more, we wonder why we did not spend more time in this region when we were younger, travelling through Europe in our Volkswagen Combi van.

Unlike this tandem journey, where we pick up travel brochures and decide what tourist sites to visit as we go along; back in our youth we did have a guide book and a vehicle. 'Europe on $10 a Day' by Arthur Frommer was followed religiously, both for the places of interest recommended, as well as in trying to restrict our spending to the budget boasted in the title. In fact, we were so stingy, we managed on average to live on the $10 a day between the two of us!

Our frugality included sleeping in secluded places, rather than paying for camp-grounds, and almost never buying ice-cream, beer or any other treats enjoyed by other young people. Cooking all of our own meals was a huge saving, especially when many were as simple as prizing open a can, and heating the contents of one of the Heinz products we carried. We had purchased case loads of unlabelled cans, at the staff-discount price of threepence each, from the Heinz factory shop. Stowed away under the seats, they had been used regularly during the early part of our travel, as we drove through the most expensive Scandinavian countries. The only clue to a can's contents was a code embossed on the lid, which we had often forgotten; some of our meals were a lucky dip. Our taste for baked beans dissipated long before our supplies were exhausted. Much later into our travels we were able to sell off the excess cans of beans to young Englishmen travelling through Greece, who were craving for what could almost have been considered England's 'staple' dish.

The reward for our thriftiness was to be able to travel, over four summer months, along a route that took us where and when we pleased. Our journey from the UK had taken us through Belgium and Holland, to Scandinavia for brief visits to Denmark, Norway and Sweden. Driving across Europe included travel through the German Federal Republic, Austria, Hungary, Yugoslavia and Bulgaria, into Turkey, the eastern most point of our travel. Returning to the UK was a relaxed drive taking in the sites of Greece, Italy, Spain and France. Our life purpose at that time was to travel, stopping in every capital city, and visiting all major tourist sites, as well as calling in at as many geographical marvels as possible along the way.

Today, is a pleasant day of riding through a picturesque corner of Provence, on a road that takes us along the forested foothills of the Plateau de Vaucluse. There is a 500 meter hill-climb to reach the small, quaint village of Murs. With a population of only 400, the stone walled houses, buildings and private castle, are devoid of colour. Later the road winds its way up the Col De Murs. The effort is rewarded with a very long descent of curving cornering and effortless leg spinning.

Our travels today take us through Vénasque, another pretty village, perched 300 meters on the summit of a rocky outcrop. The stone is again uncomplicated by colour, and appears austere. The climb is rewarded with another down-hill 'cruise', to St-Didier, nestled in the valley.

Our time of arrival at Pernes-Les-Fontaines is a civilised mid-afternoon. Pernes-Les-Fontaines is an ancient city that took its name to mark its reverence for water, and its beautiful fountains. A tourist brochure, with map, will guide us to each of the thirty-nine fountains. Finding all thirty-nine becomes our challenge for the remainder of the afternoon. This proves to be impossible in the time we have, but it gives us the opportunity to explore the streets with purpose. We locate many fountains, ranging from insignificant troughs to grand ornate features; all having a common theme; at least one water spout!

This is our final night in France, so a celebration by fine dining at a restaurant is in order. We have worked up a hearty appetite, and by 6.00 p.m. are looking for somewhere to eat. This hour is much too early for the French to dine, and we wander around looking for a restaurant that is open. La Table d'Aymee is a very small restaurant with tables el fresco. The restaurant is only open in the summer months and the kitchen, the only part of the restaurant that is indoors, is tiny; not much bigger than a narrow corridor. We sit at a table, but are told they are not open yet; the chef will not be reporting for duty until 7 o'clock. We don't mind, we are happy for the opportunity to sit and relax and enjoy the balmy evening. A little later we are offered a bottle of the house wine and sliced bread is brought to the table to accompany it. The little impromptu entrée numbs the hunger pangs until the kitchen opens and we can enjoy a meal of the local duck. In true Provencal style, the meat is topped with a rich burgundy glaze of currants and grapes, decoratively displayed in the centre of an unusual but tasty combination of morsels: mushroom, tomato, potato, grilled capsicum and fennel, garnished with orange slices and pine nuts, which I am sure will give us enough calories so that tomorrow we will easily be able to pedal the twenty-eight kilometres back to Avignon.

Celebrating our final night in France

Distance covered: 22.45 miles

Average speed: 12.4 mph

Riding time: 1 hours 47 minutes

Pernes-Les-Fontaines - Avignon

Day Six: Provence
Friday, 6th July

I t's afternoon, on a week day, when we return to Avignon. Unlike the time of our departure, last Sunday afternoon, siesta is over and the locals are going about their business. Avignon feels pulsating and vibrant as we ride through the ancient narrow streets. The dates on the posters show the arts festival is in full swing, but we won't be participating; we are heading for the station and Italy.

Our first priority is to collect our 'bike-box' and contents stored in the motel laundry. We tandem there together, but I am left to gather our belongings while Nev returns to the station, riding the tandem on his own. I will join him shortly; transporting all our gear by taxi.

Arriving at the station, I find Nev has already leaned the tandem on the exterior of the building. He is tucked around the corner from the main thoroughfare and has begun dismantling the bike. I set off to look for food to take with us on our overnight journey. I'm not overly excited about an 'all-nighter' on the train. We have not booked a sleeper and will need items for an evening meal and 'nibble-treats', to distract us from the long hours of wakefulness.

When I return, Nev's secluded position is now in the full sun. He is dripping sweat, but too intent on his task to attend to his own comfort. I insist he moves before he gets sunstroke, and join him in dragging our equipment to the shade of a tree, then help him with the packing of 'bike bits'. There is a delicate communion in the simple tasks that we perform together and the job is quickly done.

On entering the station, Nev suggests I go and get changed out of my cycling gear. I get to the bathroom and realise that I haven't got a coin to allow me to enter. This is so annoying; I forget that I have to pay almost every time when I want to use a public toilet. I return to Nev for the correct change and go back to the bathroom. I don't think I have taken long, after all there isn't much to it when just changing out of cycling gear into trousers and tee-shirt, but Nev is quite annoyed when I get back, as he will not have time to wash and change.

"Hurry up the train is going in a minute," he calls.

Rushing awkwardly with all our packed gear; boxed tandem and numerous bags, clattering down a flight of steps, dragging through a subway tunnel, and heaving up a stairway, we make it to the platform. Our pace slows as we are about to board the waiting train but are struck with a feeling that something is amiss. Sure we are running late but it seems odd that there is no-one on the platform; neither is there anyone on the train, nor are there conductors. Nev leaves me in the empty carriage, and goes to look for someone to find out what is going on. I have a sense of train movement that is vibrating through the underbelly of the station. Instantly, irrational fear overcomes me. I am afraid that the empty train will leave the platform, with me on board. I have seen in movies where characters have nimbly jumped off a moving train, deftly landing in a tuck and roll position, and I am visualising, for a split second, myself performing such a feat! No way! But the perception charges my body with shots of adrenaline, that quickly replace the notion of flight with jelly-like legs that quiver in fear of being whisked away to goodness knows where. Fortunately the train I am on remains stationary.

Nev returns, he hasn't found anyone to speak to and suggests that I go and look. If I do find someone, Nev thinks, I may at least be able to make sense of what is said. I leave Nev on the train and on inquiring of an official looking man in uniform, am advised we are on the wrong platform.

I hurry back to Nev and garble the news. The words have hardly fallen from my mouth before Nev has already hoisted the bike box onto his shoulders and rushed off. I follow him as fast as I can.

Because I overfilled my backpack with the provisions, the top zip is not fastened. My jostling and bumping down steps causes the avocado, apples and container of dip, to bounce out and fall around my feet. I am frantically trying to collect these items when a rush of people, heading for the exit or to the train we have just vacated, comes head-on towards me. I have managed to grab the groceries from beneath the pounding feet, and with produce and bags clutched tightly, I barge through this oncoming onslaught of humanity, hugging against the left-hand wall; in an automatic response learned from a life-time of keeping left, both as a driver and as a pedestrian. Not realising that I should be on the right, where I would have clear access, I am shoving through this human barrier, spluttering "Pardon, excusez moi." My head is bursting with the rush of adrenaline and the French words are mixed with a silent mantra of *'don't go without me, hurry, hurry you can't miss the train, please still be there'*.

Amid the pandemonium, a sense of déjà vu pervades. A surreal feeling that I have been in exactly this situation sometime before, slows my senses to a dreamlike state. My heart feels like it has become too heavy to pump blood to my legs. I am so afraid that Nev will get on the train, and I will be left stranded. Later, while I am recovering from this ordeal, I realise that I had been yelling exactly the words of the thoughts that had formulated in my head just days ago, in the rush for the train at Reading station!

Bursting onto the platform, my heart skips a beat as I find it deserted. A quick scan of the platform confirms I am wrong. There is no train, but a male figure is slumped on a bench-seat looking both annoyed and defeated. Thank goodness! Nev missed the train.

"We've missed it! What now?" The angry question is followed with a demanding weariness "You had better go and sort it out; I can't stand the thought of lugging all this gear back to the ticket area and then dragging it all back here to the platform. I'm exhausted!" I feel the rebuke in Nev's words, and obligingly leave to sort out the situation.

At the ticket counter, the young lady's English is limited, but I get the impression that she is telling me, we can use the same tickets and get a train to Marseille, then connect to Italy. It seems an easy, yet unusual solution, but the procedure is a bit vague. I return to Nev and relay this information. The problem is that we are not sure how we will achieve this, so I decide to go back to the ticket office for more definite information. When I explain our connection was to be to Florence she points me in the direction of International Inquiries where I am told that, today is Friday; school finishes today for the summer holiday break. The trains are full. The only way we can go by train to Florence, is to take a train to Milan tomorrow. The only seats that are available are on a First Class carriage. We will have to stay tonight in Avignon, spend tomorrow night in Milan, and then the following evening resume our journey by train to Florence, arriving at 23:45.

Because we have actually missed the train we cannot be refunded the first section of that journey. Fortunately we can get a refund on the other two intended stages of travel, not yet used, between Lyon and Florence. Because our journey is now extended to travel north to Milan, and there is also now a first class component, we must pay an additional $260AUS.

I return to Nev to relay this information. This is the third time this afternoon that I have made my way towards the train platform, and by now I am feeling stressed. I need Nev's input into making a decision. As I expect, Nev is not happy about the additional costs we face. Returning together to the ticket area Nev first confirms that we do not have any other route option by train. He then makes some phone calls inquiring whether we can hire a car. That thought is quickly dismissed, as travelling across countries, picking up a vehicle in France and leaving it in Italy, makes this too difficult. With no other option we purchase the train tickets and leave the station feeling dejected, and now with the additional problem of finding accommodation for tonight to resolve.

Our first thought is to phone the motel from which, only a couple of hours ago, we had collected our gear. Yes; they have a room but it is more expensive than the one we last stayed in. Okay we will take it. Standing in the station entranceway, surrounded by our packed gear, we are confronted with the fact that we are worn out and really cannot be bothered with figuring out how we are going to lug everything to the motel. We had not asked the proprietor to come and collect us in his little van, so it was up to us to trundle the tandem, as well as get at least one taxi. Then we would have to bring everything back here tomorrow. In our present mood, the transporting of luggage dilemma seems to have escalated to monumental proportions.

Nev notices a hotel just one hundred meters away, across the car park. Fortunately the Ibis Hotel, conveniently located right next to the station has a reasonably priced room. The pre-booked motel is cancelled on the pretext that we have now been able to catch a train today after all.

As we settle for a night's sleep, that I am sure is going to be far more comfortable, than what would have been experienced on an all-night journey in an upright seat, on the overnight train that we had missed; Nev tells me he feels he really must blame himself for us having missed the train. He is struggling with the additional expense of first class train fares and two additional night's accommodation. Tonight's hotel booking substitutes an all night upright seat on the train and tomorrow we will stay in a hotel in Milan, when we had already booked, and paid for, accommodation in Southern France. "That's nonsense," I respond, "there is no need for blame, and anyway we have now got it all sorted."

Distance covered: 16 miles.

Average speed: 11.6 mph.

Riding time: 1 hours 37 minutes

Avignon – Milan

Saturday, 7th July

From the Avignon Post Office we parcel all our wet weather gear to send home; in regard to the weather at least, we are feeling optimistic! Travel treats have been purchased and we have enjoyed a picnic breakfast in the city gardens, with the strains from a nearby church organ providing an unrelated and rather incongruent accompaniment to a troupe of Japanese people, practising their Arts Festival mime performance.

Back at the hotel room, we reorganise our packing. Our arrival at Milan is going to be late. We have decided to take the hassle out of looking for accommodation on arrival, by pre-booking the Milan Hotel Ibis. Our intention will be to leave most of our gear in storage at Milan station; taking with us only one small pannier and the small day-pack to the hotel. We are hoping that with a light load, we can explore Milan tomorrow and enjoy the result of our misadventure.

The train departs at 12:30 p.m. We are ready, and an hour early! For both of us our stress levels are at the extreme. Waiting in the foyer of Avignon station, we are constantly reviewing the tickets and scanning the departure board. I sing in my head 'When you walk through a storm, keep your head up high' to try and remain calm. I have had good results at the dentist with this block-out method, singing words learned in high school assemblies; the song is an effective focus, that allows me to mentally remove myself from an uncomfortable situation.

Problems are expected, as Nev has looked at a timetable and this train is not listed as one that carries cycles. Our tickets identify that we are in carriage number four, but we don't have seat numbers. Does this indicate we will have to sit wherever there is a vacant seat? We are all set, ready to run, and as the train advances, I notice the cycle symbol on carriage number two. We dash for that carriage; stow the carton and bags and plonk into empty seats. As the train pulls away we look at each other, smiling smugly as if partners in crime, rather than just regular train catchers; we are moving; there is nothing that can go wrong now!

We have a two hour wait in Lyon. There is nothing of interest here, as we had explored the station only a week ago. Our connection arrives, and we rush as usual and soon find our first class seats. Beautifully upholstered, the seats are wide and comfortable, and we settle back to enjoy the picturesque landscape. The journey takes us through corn fields and forests, alongside sparkling mountain lakes and beneath the snow capped peaks of the French Alps, through the town of Chambéry towards Italy.

We are almost at the Italian border, at the town of Modane, where the train stops and all passengers are to disembark the TGV train. Another train will come to take us further, we are told, and we are to cross the platform in readiness to board it. Further instruction indicates we will board the same carriage number and seat number, as the train we have just disembarked; there are no further announcements.

Hundreds of people wait on the platform overlooked by mountain peaks and a fine castle ruin. There is little conversation; instead a palpable feeling that something is 'not quite right' pervades. A woman asks a guard 'what time does the other train arrive', and I catch the reply of seven-something. She appears rather worried; I know that feeling well. This time though, we are relaxed, as we have no other connections.

The wait extends long past what we are expecting, and we begin to feel abandoned. That is not a sensible thought, as the train we arrived on, hasn't left. We figure the Italian train will get here eventually, and its passengers will transfer to the train we have disembarked from and it will return to France, and we will board the train they just vacated, and head for Italy.

One hour later the Italian train arrives. We have left carriage twelve and this train does not have a number twelve. I ask a man in uniform and he explains that if we were on twelve then the new carriage is two; and so it was. Seats 72 and 73 are easily found, however we have only just seated ourselves when we are approached by an English couple who also have the same seat numbers. I guess this may be a problem with a double-decker train converting to one? We suggest they enquire of the conductor, and they later pop their heads in to let us know that 'it was sorted.' Thank goodness! I really don't want any more train travel problems!

This train is much less luxurious, but nevertheless we ease back into the seat and relax as the journey continues through the beautiful mountain scenery, interrupted only by an occasional tunnel.

It's easy to follow the signs to the Milan Centrale luggage room. We have full view of an enormous room. This looks really hopeful as we spy layers of shelves displaying an array of left luggage and no lockers to squeeze too many items into. It will be wonderful, at the very least, to leave the bike, so that we can walk easily to the Ibis Hotel that we know, while central, is still about one and a half kilometres away. Waiting at the counter is a lesson in patience. It is 10:00 p.m. and the luggage room is supposed to be open until a much later hour. There is no attendant in sight and no bell to press for attention.

"Ah, there's someone. Down the back there, looks like he works here." Nev hopes.

We call out, but are unable to attract the man's attention. When he finally does make the effort to come to the counter, there are at least a dozen other people waiting with us. Nev is instructed to put the bike box on the scales. It weighs more than the twenty kilo maximum. The man points to a sign on the wall by the scales, and then speaking in Italian, punctuated with hand gesticulations, makes it quite clear, that a luggage minder employed at this station, is not allowed to lift any weight over twenty kilos. Nev, using sign language to help translate his English, offers to go around to the other side of the counter and lift the box himself. No such luck! That is not allowed; customers must remain this side of the counter! The bike box does not comply with the regulations. We have no choice but to take our burden with us.

Sharing the 'lugging of the box', the one item we wanted so desperately to leave behind, we take our respective positions on alternate sides of the carton, pulling it across the cobbled square, bumping it up and down pavements as we make our way to the Ibis Centrale.

From bed we are able to catch the late television news, before sleep overcomes us. Today the Tour de France started in London. We have often contemplated a trip to France to follow the tour, but in our rush to get organised for this holiday, had failed to realise that we would be in Europe when the event was held this year. Today we left Provence where many stages of Le Tour are held. We cannot believe that now we are in Italy and have missed being in the right place to fulfil another dream; by just a few days!

Milan - Florence

Sunday, 8th July

Milan; our unplanned visit to the city, is beginning to feel exciting although we only have a few hours to enjoy it. The tourist brochures we have looked at only make us wish that we could have had longer here, but a vehicle would have been needed to explore the wider mountain area of Lake Como. This region is added to the list of places to return to; maybe in our retirement.

Out early, keen to make the most of the time we have here, today we will visit the city-centre sites, by way of our usual, on-foot, self-guided tour. Something to eat is first on the tour schedule. There is nothing more flamboyant than the preparation of a breakfast in the Italian style. Taking high stools and eating at a shelf on the perimeter of a café, our space to the side of the general bustle is a great spot to watch the entertaining antics of a barista. He delights in his own performance, as he daintily tosses the cups, two at a time, of freshly brewed coffee, to land delicately on the saucers. The atmosphere is perfumed with the coffee aroma and the enticing smell of hot croissants. Customers pop in for their morning 'fix'; stopping only long enough to gulp the espresso in one 'toss of liquid' down the throat. Cash is exchanged for the coffee, as well as for a hot croissant wrapped in a paper napkin, that they take to 'eat-on-the-run'.

A three kilometre walk takes us to Parco Semipione. The park is made up of huge expanses of lawn; divided by myriads of curving pathways that surround gardens, thickets of shrubbery and ornamental ponds. We are enjoying the hot summer's morning along with hundreds of other people. There are energetic people jogging, families cycling together or picnicking, and many groups of Asian people dressed casually in jeans and tee-shirts that are surrounding blushing, gowned brides and formally dressed grooms, posing for photographs. We are amused by the number of bridal parties, having never before seen so many weddings being performed in one place. Yesterday was Saturday the 7th of July 2007. Asian cultures believe that number seven is a lucky number for relationships, symbolising togetherness. Today 8/7/07 may be even luckier, as number eight represents prosperity and good fortune. Prosperity and togetherness; no wonder so many have chosen today to perform their nuptials.

While I am gazing in awe at the colossal cathedral at the far end of the Piazza del Duomo, I am surprised to find my hand has been taken by a young man. He has placed dried kernels of corn in my palm, enclosing my fingers over the seeds so that I do not drop them. I look at him questioningly and he explains the corn is for the pigeons. The pigeons know this better than me and have already made their way to perch on my shoulders and flap around my outstretched arm. The man wants Nev to give him the camera. I'm beginning to feel uncomfortable; the camera was new for this trip and I'm worried that this guy wants to run off with it. He indicates that he will take a photo, which is really dumb, because Nev could do this, but he quickly shoves corn into Nev's palm and Nev too is surrounded by flapping birds. Nev passes the camera to him; photos are taken. Then the man wants some money for the corn. Not just some money, he is demanding five Euros. "You have got to be kidding; five Euro for a few seeds!" I snatch back the camera and we walk away with his demands for payment following us across the square. Realising that we have been caught in a scam, Nev yells "We didn't ask for the corn! We're not giving you any money!" We quicken our pace but the guy is so insistent that Nev gives him one Euro just to get rid of him. We cross quickly to the Duomo, mentally calculating how much money this crafty conman must earn, even if only scamming one Euro from each tourist, it would be a profitable venture.

The Duomo is the third largest cathedral in Europe. Construction began in 1386, and the main spire was completed in 1774. The original design was Gothic but the structure evolved, responding to the architectural influences over five centuries.

Shoulders and knees must be covered to enter, and I consider myself lucky to be able to go inside as my shorts only cover half of my kneecaps, and the tee-shirt I am wearing has a very small cap sleeve. There is a church service being held, so we steer clear of the congregation by taking the climb to the roof and the tower. From the ground the structure was very impressive, but from the roof top the architecture is marvellous. The roof gradient is a football-field size gentle slope of huge marble tiles, bordered by 135 ornate marble spires, each supporting a life-size statue of a saint, immortalised in stone. The rooftop is also a great platform from which to view the city of Milan.

Opposite the Duomo is the Galleria Vittorio Emanuele II. The Galleria is a shopping arcade, built during the years 1865 to 1877, as a link between Duomo Plaza and the Opera House Plaza. The domed-roof of glass and iron is quite spectacular and window-shopping here is as close as I am likely to get to viewing designer clothing creations. Windows display couture that is rather garish and excessively pricy, so I don't mind that shopping is not on our itinerary. Except that I have the opportunity to go to the toilet, I am nevertheless disappointed to see the fast food chain McDonalds, has a presence here.

Scammed! Piazza del Duomo, Milan

Avoiding further problematic experiences attributed to train travel is a high priority, so we head to the Ibis hotel for a quick freshen up before venturing out to look for food that we can eat on the train. Wandering around aimlessly seeking out a supermarket proves fruitless, so we head for the station without any supplies. Fortunately we notice two men carrying plastic grocery bags and they inform us that there is a supermarket in the train station!

Our departure time is 5:15 p.m. but first our stored bags need to be recovered. Nev leaves me at a platform with the tandem, while he goes to retrieve the panniers. He eventually makes his way back to me, and I suggest that he venture off again to look for the supermarket, while I stay with the luggage. Meanwhile I am searching the departure boards, trying to identify which platform we will need to embark from. My stomach becomes knotted with nerves, when I realise that the signage indicates the final stop on each line. We are heading for Florence via Pisa; both cities are part-way down the country, and therefore not listed as an end of line destination. We do not have a map of Italy and the names displayed are meaningless. Nev returns empty handed, throwing a few words in my direction, which I fail to catch. Even as he is speaking, he is moving away again. I don't even have the chance to tell him of my concern, as he immediately rushes off in another direction.

My apprehension is distracted by the sight of a cat, in collar, with loose leash trailing. The cat's hair is electrified to bristle-stiff erectness, and with eyes widely startled, the animal runs frantically between legs. I crouch to ground level and call gently, "Here Puss, Puss, Puss," whilst trying to catch the leash. The atmosphere is too overwhelming, for the cat and me both. I can stay rooted in my fear, waiting for my companion to return, but the bewildered cat disappears, frantically skittering amongst legs and luggage.

I've studied the tickets and notice there is no seat number printed. I wonder, *'do we authenticate the ticket before boarding?'* Two trains are scheduled to depart at the same time as that printed on our ticket but there is no train number listed. The travel folder I hold only shows a map of France. *'Do we go to Lirenzo?'* There is no mention of Pisa, where we are to transfer to another line to Florence. Nev returns with groceries and I explain my fears. He hurries off again, this time to seek information.

Rushing towards me, with angst written all over his face, Nev is yelling "Platform 21 leaves in five minutes." Our train is not scheduled until 17:15 but Nev is wound up like the 'Energizer Bunny', hoisting the tandem onto a trolley and already on the run. I've responded to his urgency and run beside the trolley while throwing on the rest of the bags. We leap onto the trolley ourselves, 'scooting' along, in an effort to cover the huge distance, from platform four to twenty-one, as quickly as possible.

Even as we rush towards the platform, I'm still not convinced this is right. Nev insists that at the information office they were clear in explaining that this would be the right train. He shows me that the man he spoke with has written a new time on his ticket. There is a train waiting, and Nev confirms from the official working on the platform that, yes, this train is going to Pisa.

We are seated on board, still puffing from the exertion of rushing, when the train guard asks about our box. My heart rate elevates higher, but the guard moves along and I relax again. The train moves off slowly, we are hardly moving when the guard returns to check our ticket. The guard studies the ticket intently for a drawn-out moment, and then suggests "There is a faster train going to Pisa, leaving at 17:15." That is obviously the train we were expecting to travel on but it is too late for us, we are already rolling. The guard advises that we will arrive in Florence at 21:50. While a little later than the other train, we will still be able to pick up the connection to Florence at 22:30.

Nev pulls two cold Heinekin beers from his bag and suggests we drink to yet another misadventure. The tab is snapped; I am about to take a swig when the guard returns. I jump guiltily, thinking we mustn't be allowed alcohol on the train. "Are you able to change a ten Euro note into smaller notes?" he asks. I guess he thinks that, as tourists, we may be carrying a variety of notes and coinage. We are actually able to oblige.

If I am going to avoid a premature coronary I need to relax. With five hours on the train, I settle back to make the most of the journey. Our neighbour across the aisle is accompanied by a little pooch. Dogs are allowed to travel free providing they are caged. The little Chihuahua is popped back into the cage at any sign of a train official. At other times the dog sits on the ladies lap, or mooches around under the seats. The carriage is uncomfortably hot. Windows are lowered to provide natural air conditioning, but there is almost no benefit, as the breeze is carried on warm air currents. The train is thudding along at a slow pace. With shudders and pulsations, it seems to be limping along, and it stops at many stations. It is apparent that we had rushed for a slow, low class of train when we had paid for an air-conditioned fast one!

I had spoken to Mili yesterday, when I rang to tell her we would not be arriving in Florence on the early morning train as expected, but would now be arriving the same day, but at fifteen minutes to midnight. She explained that she would meet us on the street outside the station. I am a little worried about this, as I am wondering how she will transport us to her guest house. We have been waiting for a while and I decide to phone her again. I was expecting someone in a car but Mili is actually standing only 100 meters away and seems a little annoyed that I have not understood her instructions. We have not come out of the station via the exit she had told me she would meet us at.

No transport is required as the guest house we are to stay at is across the pedestrian crossing, directly over the road from the station. Mili shows us to a large room with a high ornate ceiling and patterned mosaic floor. There are two bathrooms and a well equipped kitchen that we will share with other guests. Nev notices a small central internal courtyard outside the kitchen and Mili agrees that it will be okay for the bike box to be left there for us to collect on Friday.

Florence - Radda in Chianti

Day One: Tuscany
Monday, 9th July

For the last time on this holiday, Nev erects the tandem. The bike is ready and waiting in the hallway when I get up out of bed. Before we mount though, we have four hours, on foot, to explore Florence. We know this will not be long enough to enjoy any more than a cursory wander around the city centre and a visit to only one of the many tourist attractions. At 9.30 a.m. there is already a long line of people queuing at the tourist ticket office, waiting for the office to open at 10. Later we notice that by 10:30 the queue to enter the Duomo is already 150 meters long.

My only memory of our last visit to Florence is of spending a long time gazing in awe at Michelangelo's art, particularly of David. Over the years, photos have reminded me of the river scene, particularly looking towards the bridge Ponte Vecchio which was the only one of the ancient bridges of Florence not destroyed by the Germans in 1944. This time we will miss the statuary but will make our way to Ponte Vecchio later in the morning. Right now we are at the head of the queue and ready to enter the Basilica di Santa Maria del Fiore.

The grand cathedral is the largest in Italy. Building began in 1296 and it took over 140 years to complete the structure; however the external façade, following various periods of building and dismantling, was not completed until 1887. The building exterior is very decorative; made of marble panels, of varying shades of pink and green, laid between white marble in ornate vertical and horizontal panels. The final, crowning glory is the dome of terracotta, with eight white ribs, which towers above the other Florentine buildings.

We are running out of time, as we need to leave Florence early afternoon, so hurry through the narrow streets to Ponte Vecchio, the medieval stone arched bridge across the River Arno. The bridge has always hosted shops, and these days they are predominantly jewellers, artisans, and souvenir shops. A tiny silver tandem displayed in a silversmith's window catches my attention. Small enough to put away in a pannier, we agree to purchase the trinket, as a fitting memento of our trip.

It's one of the hottest days we have had and the heat, along with our rushing around, is wearying. Walking around and around the same city block, trying to find a little narrow shop we had seen this morning that sells groceries, our discussion becomes tetchy. We both have different ideas of where the shop was located, and in spite of searching in each possible area, we are not able to locate it. I'm beginning to feel frustrated, and insist we forget it and move on.

There is a choice of route to our destination today. The map shows the first road we will come to, and the most obvious choice, will be the road towards Greve, following a valley. We will not, therefore, need to be at all concerned about how to get to the alternative route that, when it heads south, clearly involves some climbing. We leave Florence via the ring road; fortunately there is a cycle track bordering the wide traffic filled avenues. Nev is obviously irritated because I insist we stay on the cycle track. "After all," I admonish, "the intention would be that bikes travel on the track because they will be safer away from the vehicles." From my point of view, riding the cycle tracks is a non-negotiable option. Nev has, many times on this trip, expressed his distaste for them. Nev doesn't believe cycle lanes are as safe as being out on the road. He reckons he has to keep his wits about him, especially with the constant crossing of side roads, and is concerned about being hit side-on. Riding the bike lane, or not, has been one point of difference that we have argued about. I have noticed that the general layout of the streets is very systematic, having a one-way side-road coming into the avenue, and the next side road one-way away from the avenue. To me, checking what the traffic may be doing is not too complicated; simply a turn of the head in either direction.

Our only other major point of difference, regarding cycling that is, is riding around multi-lane roundabouts. Nev likes to take what he considers to be his rightful place out in the flow of traffic. I feel totally freaked out; my panic probably impacting on the tandem's turning capabilities. Nev usually gives-in to my vulnerabilities by pulling over, so we can walk, however he delights in pointing out what he believes to be the stupidity of the decision, at each of the three or more points, intersected by roads, where we need to give way to oncoming or departing traffic, before negotiating a crossing.

The Viale Michaelangelo has a smooth tarmac surface and we gently climb. I am easily distracted from the cycling task, as all the while I am trying to catch glimpses of the Duomo, and other rooftops, of the historic buildings of Florence which is now spread out to our right. Nev thinks we may have missed the turn-off, and we stop at a campground to confirm our position. He is right; it seems we have missed the valley turn-off by about two kilometres. One member of this 'troupe' will never turn around and double-back, especially when there is an option recovering the route, by moving in a forward direction. So Nev continues and I have no option but to follow; winding further along Viale Michaelangelo. We find ourselves back at river level, opposite the city of Florence, so have made no progress, even though we have been riding for an hour.

The map is consulted again, and we establish that taking a left-turn into the countryside from this point, will keep us off the motorway, whilst allowing us to join the original road of our intended course, later on. The left-turn is negotiated, and leads us immediately to tackle a steep climb. "What happened to the valley?" I moan as we continue to travel in an upward direction.

We know that on this impromptu route, we have to take another left-turn. We are pretty sure we should have come across it by now, but that road is also elusive. Not expecting to have gone through San Felice we stop to ask for directions. Our fears are confirmed; another navigational error! Fortunately at least we only have to back-track just a little to the piazza. The road we need is accessible from the square; running parallel, in the same direction we are travelling, but from the square's west side and we hadn't noticed any signage.

Thank goodness this time we have not gone too far before recovering our position.

Living in Adelaide we have been exposed to extreme summer temperatures, often in the high thirties Celcius. I find that physically I don't cope very well exercising in heat, so avoid any strenuous activity if the temperature exceeds thirty. Today is exceptionally hot and we are thirstier than we have ever been. All of the water we carry has been drunk within the first hour of cycling. We are travelling on a hill roller-coaster. Many of the hill climbs are steep, and Nev is just dropping into granny gear straight off, no request from me, and no comments from him anymore about 'hills having to earn respect'. This is our first day on the tandem after a three day break, we are tired already and wondering if we could have lost our fitness so soon.

This region is the picturesque home of Chianti. The scenery is beautiful. Gentle rolling hills blanketed with patchworks of grape vines, straight lines of lush summer greenery, that contrast with the sage of olive groves and the signature Cyprus trees; tall sentinels defining driveways and boundaries around grand mansions. Washed blues, mist distant hills, that look rather more intimidating than the undulations surrounding us; thankfully we are not travelling in that direction.

The hills become much steeper in gradient and longer in distance to the top. We are urged on by the cacophony of the cicada chorus. A road sign indicates we are going to climb now, for three winding kilometres, and warns that we could be faced with slippery conditions, snowflakes and thunderstorms! Clearly these are winter warnings; inclement weather is not going to affect us today.

The temperature was thirty-four degrees when we left Florence at midday. In this exposed rural setting the air is hot, and the black tarmac is radiating additional heat. The exertion that I am feeling, from hill climbing, is compounded by the hot air temperature, causing my body to react; face and feet feeling hot and tight as if they are about to explode. I have been in this same situation in the past, when I have been running, or mountain biking, on excessively hot days. My body just cannot seem to cool. Thoughts of whether there is any truth in the stories of the human body internally combusting, go through my mind. I try to visualise cool thoughts. My favourite is that I am lying beside Lake Taupo in New Zealand. This central North Island lake is fed by the melting winter snow, and is always extremely cold. I visually dive into the lake's chilly depths and try to cool my burning skin. My thoughts are flickering from one subject to another, focusing on anything that will remove me from the present reality. A quirky expression of my mother's, pops into my mind. The thought that *'the next time my mother sees me I'll be in a box'* - the odd sort of thing she would say!

I don't believe it! Having covered the three kilometre climb, we are now riding level ground for 200 meters. At the end of that short distance we can already see from this position, the next road sign warning of another two kilometre winding climb. I begin to curse that we missed our first preferred route choice. That road is a few kilometres west of here; and I am convinced it will be following a valley road, presumably flat, from Florence.

We stop at Strada, purchasing two litres of water that is quickly guzzled. An hour later we are thirsty again, the liquid supplies are depleted, as are my energy levels. A reward is due. An icy treat at Cintoia will improve the situation, but we have overlooked that siesta also interrupts the Italian retail industry, and find that the only grocery store open at this time, sells packaged ice-creams.   Only good quality gelati will suffice and we are prepared to be patient.   With a purchase made here, of only more water, we are keen to move on, and hopefully catch up with our preferred treat at the next village. I notice, as I open the plastic container, that there is a faint hiss and that we have purchased mineral water *'fissanete'*.   I fill the water bottles and stow them in their cages.   Just on the outskirts of the town we notice a gelati shop that is open, so stop to enjoy our preferred treat.

Within ten minutes we are back on the bike and resume climbing. I am beginning to feel overwhelmed by the heat again, and reach down for the water bottle. With the bottle secure in my hand and clenching the bottle nipple in my teeth, I pull. The pressure that has built up in the bottle, from the expansion of the heated aerated water, causes a liquid jet to squirt straight down my throat, into my lungs. I double over in a fit of coughing and spluttering. It seems I am to survive the heat only to be overcome by 'death through choking'. Nev pulls to a stop and I double over at the side of the road retching and dribbling; the regurgitated mineral water burning my throat. Eventually the sensation of asphyxiation subsides and I return to my position as 'stoker', on the back of the bike.

Our destination this evening will be Villa Sant'Uberto, Radda in Chianti.   Being rather more expensive than we would usually want to pay, we figured that as we would be coming towards the end of our travel, we would deserve some luxury, and so this accommodation was to be our holiday treat. Two nights had been booked, but having had our unexpected stopover in Milan we will now have only one night there. It is 6.00 p.m. when we arrive. Plans for the evening are to cool in the pool, imbibe some of the famous wines of the Chianti region, and partake of a gourmet dinner in the restaurant. On checking-in though, we are disappointed to hear that, even though we had cancelled last night's accommodation in advance, it had not been in the stipulated time-frame of forty-eight hours' notice. There is unfortunately no chance of a refund, so we will have to forfeit the full cost of that one night's fee that we have paid in advance. There is also no restaurant. There is a restaurant directly next door; however, today being Monday, is the only day of the week that the restaurant is not open. If we want to eat tonight, we are faced with the prospect of a three kilometre gently undulating ride that will take us to the nearest restaurant at Castellina in Chianti, followed by the return trip.

In the meantime we are shown to a large, luxurious, first floor room, which is elegantly furnished in the typical Tuscan style, with wrought iron bed, and with adjoining en-suite. The proprietor flamboyantly opens the doors leading to our private balcony, exposing a view overlooking the countryside.

To cool the body, and temper the disappointment of having lost money, as no refund will be made, and to simmer the frustration of now finding ourselves at the end of the day with no food; we head to the pool. Nev mutters about demanding that they serve us the breakfast that we have had to pay for, and would have eaten this morning, had we been here.

Biking further kilometres today, along unfamiliar narrow country roads, that are soon to be enveloped in darkness, is not something that either of us wants to do. The decision is made that, after our swim, we will ask the staff if they would make us some sandwiches. While walking back to our room Nev stops to speak to an American couple, who happen to look up and call "Hi!" Brian and Laura are just finishing a meal at the picnic table outside their ground floor apartment. The three are soon in animated conversation, which includes Nev telling them of our plight, and results in an invitation for us to join them. Not being too proud to 'bludge'; we duly purchase from the bar, a bottle of the local vino to share, and seating ourselves at their table, eat the Pasta and Sauce left over from their meal. What a pleasant evening we spend with this honeymoon couple. They have an apartment with a kitchen and Brian has been displaying his culinary prowess by being the pasta cook, and he has even baked home-made bread. I am ready to trade-in Nev for a newer, kitchen talented, version of a husband.

Distance covered: 22.45 miles.

Average speed: 12.4 mph.

Riding time: 1 hours 47 minutes

Radda in Chianti - San Gimignano

Day Two: Tuscany
Tuesday, 10th July

Breakfast for us, is a 'got to get our money's worth' feast. There is only one other couple in the dining room this early. Their accent identifies them as Canadian, and they look similar in age to us. Discussion between our two tables establishes that they are also on a cycling holiday. They have 'Bike Friday' cycles that have been made specifically for their individual size and height. Apart from espousing the comfort of the riding position, their cycles can also fold quite small and be stowed in a suitcase for travelling. Guide notes, that they have no further need of, covering the journey from San Gimignano to Siena, are given to us. They highly recommended that we follow the printed route when we travel in that direction tomorrow.

Yesterday's climbing is now being rewarded with a blissful downhill ride, for much of the thirty-four kilometres to Poggibonsi. There is a pleasurable rhythm as the tandem dances gently, swaying from side to side, while negotiating the tight switchbacks of a dizzying descent. With gravity in our favour, riding is easy and, knowing I am heading closer to our date to head home, I feel as excited as I have ever been on this holiday. The road is narrow, and we hug the verge of the right-hand

It is best to be prepared for many challenges.

side giving us the widest 'girth' to turn into blind corners. We have dropped almost to the bottom of the valley, and just about to hang a sharp left, when we come head to head with a juggernaut. The truck driver is trying to negotiate, what is from his perspective, a tight right-hand bend. With limited road width the truck is taking up the entire sweep of the corner. I yell out a long drawn guttural "Whoa!" Nev squeezes the brakes, and I clutch the handlebars as he pulls us instantly into a crawl, leaving the hard tarmac and onto the gravel edge. Neither my screeching, nor my pulling on the rear handlebars, does anything to assist Nev in avoiding potential tragedy. Nev is calm and controlled and I am staring at the driver's face as we squeeze past the truck with a hairline margin for error. "Nothing to worry about," Nev responds to my display of fear. "He didn't want to hit us anymore than we wanted to be under his wheels!" And with that statement uttered, Nev continues to lead us nonchalantly, as if nothing untoward happened.

Poggibonsi gives us our only experience of a European outdoor market. It is 11.45 a.m. and the market is bustling with women making purchases for lunch. We seek out fillings and fruit, to accompany the bread rolls we buy. Mozzarella di Bufala, olives and red ripe tomatoes, are fresh delights for a picnic feast to be enjoyed later. Hot roasted potatoes are fortifying carbohydrates that are eaten immediately.

Onwards and upwards now, we cycle to San Gimignano, a village that was designated a UNESCO World Heritage Site in 1990, and, as is the nature of ancient villages, sprawls atop a hill. Hilltop building sites provided fortification in this area which has a long ancient history of clan rivalries. San Gimignano was known historically as the city of one hundred towers. These were built as a display of great wealth, financed with the income from 'the golden spice', saffron. There were once, seventy-two towers, built in the 1200s. Of those towers, fifteen have withstood time.

It is our intention to go directly to the Information Centre, get directions to our accommodation for tonight, check-in, stow our luggage and spend the afternoon exploring. On our arrival at the centre of the ancient village, at two minutes past one o'clock, we find that the Tourist Information office is closed for siesta, from one until three every day, as is the museum and other points of interest! With the main attractions closed, there is nothing else for tourists to do. Many people are loitering in the main square. One man has a very large guide book of San

Gimignano and environs, and he is happy to search in it for directions to Casolare di Remignoli, but cannot find a listing. I call the phone number that has been included in the e-mail stored in our PDA, but I do not speak Italian, and the English response is heavily accented and I am unable to get a clear understanding of where to go. We have no option but to stay for a couple of hours.

Cycling through narrow cobbled streets, takes us away from the heat of the exposed, sun scorched central piazza. On the outskirts of the village, we find a small square, totally shaded by an ancient tree. A shaded park bench provides an ideal spot for us to rest and enjoy our picnic lunch. A woman occupies the other park bench, sprawled out in siesta induced repose. We chat quietly but she is soon disturbed and takes herself away.

Weaving through the maze of narrow streets, we explore the village, until three o'clock, when the tourist staff will be back at work. The lady at the information centre explains our accommodation is actually not in the village, but out in the country, just ten minutes' drive away. We hadn't realised that we had chosen a rural setting, so decide to continue our exploration of the village and museum now, as tomorrow we will be heading away in a southerly direction.

Ten minutes by car, as with most tourist distances, is probably an under estimation. By bicycle, the ride to our accommodation is much further than we anticipated. We have deviated away from the scenic route and are now negotiating narrow, gravel country roads, that undulate and twist; our first test of the mountain-bike capabilities of the tandem. Casolare di

Remignoli is an ancient farmhouse, restored to retain the wooden beams and terracotta floors. Set apart from the main farmhouse, our rustic room, with ensuite, is very private. Breakfast is served in the dining room or on the terrace; there is however, no restaurant.

We have been caught out again. At seven kilometres from San Gimignano we are more rural than we expected to be, and there is no food here. There is a pool and we relax in the cool water. From where we float, the view extends across lush rolling farmland and the Chianti vineyards, toward the walls, towers and terracotta roofs of San Gimignano on the horizon.

The small 'break' has revived our muscles and we now feel ready to tackle a ride to seek out food for our evening meal. Not wanting to back-track we steer the tandem towards Ulignano. Surprisingly, the distance is covered quickly and the ride is enjoyable. This village consists of one very short main street; there is only one shop that sells provisions. The decision on what to purchase is easy, as there is very little selection: a packet of pasta, a tomato sauce and a bottle of local red to wash the meal down.

Back at the farmhouse we set our provisions out on the picnic table beside the pool. Adding to the produce are the other supplies left over from our lunch-time picnic: a delicious buffalo mozzarella, avocado and fresh tomatoes, dinner is prepared. Far from being spoiled by the variety of European meals purchased to date, we both comment on the freshness of the flavours, savouring the memorable home cooked feast, created atop the picnic table on our little Pocket Rocket stove.

Next morning we have a small difficulty when it is time to depart. The fee is much larger than we expect and the young lady insists that we present our paper to show the amount that we were quoted. We did not carry any paper but can show her the email displayed on the PDA screen for her to read. She is not happy with the technology and neither are we happy with her insistence to pay the higher amount. It transpires that the deposit we paid went directly to the booking company and has not been forwarded to them. She was rather insistent that we should now pay the full amount including the deposit. Needless to say we paid what we considered due and left, but it put rather a damper on what had been a lovely stay. We have learned from this experience that it is best to, whenever possible, book accommodation directly with the provider.

Distance covered: 29 miles.

Average speed: 12.2 mph.

Riding time: 2 hours 33 minutes

San Gimignano - Siena

Day Three: Tuscany
Wednesday, 11th July

I t is our last day on the tandem, and we are following the guide notes, given to us by the Canadians, that will take us to Siena. The first recommendation is a stop at Val D'Elsa. This medieval village has a beautifully preserved ancient centre that is, at its highest point; accessed up a steep stair climb, from the massive car park. Unlike San Gimignano the car park is devoid of tourist buses. There are few locals about and, as we wander in the heat, we catch strains of television voices in the same diction and tone of a program such as 'Days of Our Lives'. We have the small town virtually to ourselves; and with fewer tourists, the cost of coffee and food is set at an enticingly low price. There is quirky art work displayed here that adds a comical theme; a statue of a man peeing on a wall, down a narrow lane, causes us to glance twice to confirm that it is in fact not real, and we share the lookout, at the hilltop, with a life-like statue of a young couple passionately kissing.

Sunflowers have nodded their bright yellow heads at us as we have ridden in this region and I realise I have not taken a photo of them. At this time of the day the flowers have their 'backs' to me. I do not want the road in my shot, so push my way between the stalks until I am partway into the field. Ahead of me the field is bathed in sunshine, and as I turn to capture the flowers' sunny disposition, I see that in contrast, my shot is to be framed by black clouds engorged with moisture, which threaten to drench us before our next destination. The hilltop lookout post of Monteriggioni, built to alert Siena of warmongering Florentines, though diminished by distance, is clearly defined by the stone walls and towers that encircle the village. I call to Nev to look behind him. It is highly unlikely that we are going to remain dry today!

The gathering clouds continue to warn us of a soaking, and with the loss of the Tuscan sun, the day has turned cool, so we cut short our visit to Monteriggioni.

With only ten kilometres of cycling left to complete the riding on this European section of this cycle-tour holiday, we are finishing in the same climatic conditions as the UK section. The rain has finally caught us and without rain-gear we surrender to a drenching.

We do not have a map of Siena, so it is handy that at the entrance to each side road, a large sign lists the names of all of the accommodation down that way. Slowing at each sign we check carefully to see if our hostel is listed. We haven't located our accommodation and find ourselves quickly approaching a large roundabout on the edge of the city.

Even though Nev is 'leading' and always looking straight ahead, he appears to be blinkered and doesn't notice road signs. On this occasion I happen to have my head down for a moment. Often my head is lowered as I study a map, but right now I don't have a map, so it was remiss of me not to remain focused. I catch a glimpse of the signs displayed above the road, but too late to read them, take them in and be able to orientate us in the right direction.

Our final hour of cycling is going to be in a shower of rain

We are on the roadside verge, in our usual temporary pause mode; I am seated and Nev is straddling the bar to maintain balance. We are at a loss to know what direction to take; as we have missed the road names and where they are leading to. The traffic has built up. I am not sure what direction leads towards the city, and Nev doesn't have a clue either. There are five roads to choose from. We could about-turn and approach the sign board again, but even if we 'stuck' to the verge, that is not a wise move on this busy road. Heavy traffic, coupled with a roundabout, means I am feeling anxious again and I am also annoyed about missing the signage.

As is a typical demand from me, in negotiating roundabouts, I am insistent that we dismount to walk. Nev as usual is reluctantly obliging. I know that Nev is 'brassed-off' as he is rattling off all the same arguments that I have heard so many times before. We continue to circuit, and with strained consideration, try to make the right decision about what route to take. We are ready, seated on the bike, just about to cycle away from the kerb when I happen to glance up. There is a sign advertising a radio station, and beneath it the hostel sign we have been looking for! Our walked circuit around the traffic island, and the fifty meters beyond, as luck would have it, has brought us directly outside our accommodation. Except for the short distance we will ride in two days' time, from the hostel to the railway station; this cycling journey is rather abruptly, over.

Distance covered: 21 miles.

Average speed: 10.8 mph.

Riding time: 2 hours

Siena

Day Four: Tuscany
Thursday, 12th July

The tourist brochure that we are following to explore the Comune Di Siena, is promoting a seven kilometre urban trek. Urban Trekking (walking) is espoused as a new and entertaining way to get to know the history and artistic beauty of the city; for us, to be on foot is the logical method for city exploration.

Siena is a medieval city enclosed within a circle of massive walls. The city is built on three hills and the conglomeration of stone buildings is divided by steep winding alleyways. The heart of the city, is Piazza del Campo; the huge semi-circular expanse, paved in a herringbone pattern of bricks, is bordered by a solid wall of building facades, including the town hall with its magnificent clock tower.

We've quickly worn ourselves out wandering the streets, in the heat, and head back towards the main tourist area for lunch. The narrow street we are in is for pedestrians only, but we can see that the congestion we find ourselves amongst is caused by a car ahead, that is driving at walking pace. By the time we are alongside the vehicle, we see that some of the people, crowded immediately beside the car, are gesticulating wildly. The car is transporting a bride to the nearby cathedral and it appears someone may have had their foot run over. The vehicle has stopped, and the crowd moves away from the door as it is swung open. The bride steps out, lifts up the train of her dress and flings it over her elbow. Walking unsteadily in high heels on the cobbled surface she totters her way towards the cathedral, leaving the driver to deal with the problem. I hope the incident is not a bad omen for her marriage!

Nev has been suffering from hunger lately and is keen to try the smorgasbord lunch we saw advertised yesterday. I know that I won't get my money's worth, but reckon Nev's appetite will make up for what mine lacks.

With stacked plates of food before us, we are chatting idly, when Nev decides to 'mix' a complaint into the conversation. He has found his companion lacking. Now I think I could probably sympathise if he remarked about the difficulties he has experienced, having to ride the tandem at a level that suits me, rather than his superior level of fitness. I think I would try to understand if he spoke along the lines of, me not pulling my weight on the tandem. But no; he proceeds to tell me how he has been pondering about our missed train in Avignon. Having gone over the scenario a number of times, he has concluded that really it is, entirely my fault!

It would have been easier (well maybe not, but the outcome would have been better) if I had just responded with, 'Oh come on Nev. What have you been dwelling on that for. We've had a great trip and I'm really proud of our achievements. I'm not interested in taking blame. We enjoyed our unexpected stopover in Milan and yes, while missing that train added expenses we weren't expecting, it is only money, and not like we can't afford it. Get over it!'

Instead I let Nev's words strike me like a lightening bolt out of the blue. Determined not to let them singe, I throw my opinion back, fired with a staccato of profane expletives, as if they have been shot from a gun. Nev's 'armour' appears to protect him from any wounding, but a few of my shots ricochet back and strike me, so I experience the hurt two-fold. There is no truce, just a numb hollow of stubborn self-righteousness. Stupidly we are prepared to sabotage all that we have achieved together over the past six weeks by assigning blame. Gremlin-like, the mute criticisms are tucked under the blanket that night and then continue to sit between us the next morning as we travel the short distance by train back to Florence.

Outside the apartment, opposite the train station in Florence, we have telephoned Mili and explained that we would like to retrieve the bike box. It transpires that Mili's mother lives in the apartment to the left of the foyer. An elderly Italian woman unbolts the heavy street facing door that opens into a foyer, and then admits us into the apartment that we had stayed in. Nev collects the box, however he is not keen to leave the building entirely. He reckons the foyer will be an ideal place to dismantle and package the tandem. The old woman has no English but as we continue to loiter in her foyer, discussing how we can make it known to her what we would like to do, she starts flapping her arms in annoyance at us and is making it quite clear that she does not want us hanging around. We have no option but to move on.

Back outside, the pavement is teeming with people. Carefully negotiating the traffic we head back to the station to figure out what to do next. Looking from the station, back over the road that we have just crossed, I notice an underground car park building. Carefully renegotiating the traffic we move all our gear, back to the opposite side of the road. Moving down the ramp, to an area that looks like it is set aside for motorcycles, Nev begins to dismantle the tandem.

The final dismantling and packaging of the tandem, ready for the return flight to Australia

Two men are watching us from an internal office and it is only a matter of minutes before one approaches. Even though it is clear that we are pulling a bike to bits the man asks us what we are doing. It appears that the activity itself is not a problem; however he says that we cannot occupy the space where we are. Evidently to be present in this space we should have a permit. Obviously this is private property but we have been very careful not to occupy a parking space. The painted markings on the concrete floor indicate the small triangular shaped space abutting a pillar where we are spread, is really in no-mans land, however we are in no position to argue, nor do we have the language skills to do so. We are asked how long we will be, and Nev indicates that in one hour we should be out of here.

On the first occasion that Nev dismantled and packaged the tandem, in our garage at home, it had taken him three hours. On the more recent occasion, outside the Station at Avignon, with a little assistance from me, it had been one and a half hours. To have the tandem dismantled and packaged for flight, in one hour, is really putting the pressure on. This is going to have to be a team effort. Nev pilots the process, handing me pieces for wrapping, small screws to be packaged together, or parts to wipe clean. Snatched glimpses of the clock unify our resolve to win the challenge. With moments to spare, 'Team George' has won.

Rome

Friday, 13th July

This afternoon we have another train journey, and tonight will be our final night in Europe. We are to have twelve hours in Rome. Rome is one of the cities, visited thirty-one years ago, that was etched in my memory, because of the unexpected experiences we had there. My recollection of visiting historic sites is a little hazy, although I do remember being in awe of Michelangelo's art in the Vatican.

Last time we stayed at a camping site, in our Volkswagen Combi van, on the outskirts of the city. Catching a local bus had been the easiest way to get into the city. We boarded a bus, that had standing room only, and squeezed into the crowded aisle. Not long into the ride I felt something hard pressing into my 'butt crack'. I can still remember thinking about this for some moments, trying to fathom what it could be, and the ensuing feeling of revulsion when I realised the pressure was from an 'appendage' of the male standing behind me! I cannot understand why I didn't turn around and whack the guy. Instead I whispered to Nev, making him aware of what was going on, and asking him to swap places with me. Nev was pretty protective back then, and we did a bit of a shuffle.

A little later in the day, at the time of wanting to make a purchase, we found that the earlier distraction had been an opportunity for the offender to pick my purse from my handbag. This meant that we were in the centre of Rome with no money, banks were closed and this was before the invention of the 'handy' ATM. At the railway station we begged amongst the tourists who were waiting for trains, telling of our plight and managed to scrounge sufficient value in coins for both of us to get on a bus for part of the return journey to the campsite. At some point we got kicked off the bus only to be left standing on the footpath with no idea where we were.

An elderly woman got off the bus at the same stop and she may have been trying to be helpful, but the Italian words that she repeated constantly were lost on us. We decided to walk and just about to set off, in goodness knew what direction, when we saw a group of youths coming towards us. These guys were spread across the wide pavement, loping along with teenage attitude and I became fearful that we were going to be accosted even though we had nothing of value. It was clear that my fears were going to be realised when they walked straight at us. The guy who appeared to be the leader came directly up to us. Rather than being intimidating he asked, in English with an American accent, if he could help. Evidently he had done some of his high schooling in the States. When we told him we needed to get to the campground he invited us to join them, and the group, just mates out enjoying a Saturday night, guided us all the way to the campground gates.

It was about 10:30 p.m. and dark when we finally arrived back at our camper-van, and we had not yet eaten. We were living on a shoe-string budget and every night cooked on the gas camp cooker. This night Spaghetti Bolognaise was on the menu, and while I was frying the meat and onions, thousands of mosquitos attracted to the light glow, flew into the pan as if on kamikaze attack. There was nothing I could do but stir them into the mix. When it came time to eat, I told Nev I wasn't hungry; that I was tired and felt like it was too late to eat. Months later I confessed about the mosquito bolognaise and to this day, if I ever say I don't feel hungry Nev questions "What is in this that I should know about?"

On this occasion we have settled at an inner-city hotel, and the boxed tandem is tucked safely behind a sofa in the hotel reception area. We have freedom, and determination, to jam the viewing of as many of the historic sites as possible, into the next twelve hours. We leave for the station at eight o'clock tomorrow morning. Tonight our itinerary is well planned, and with so much exploring to do, we have decided the distance we intend to cover is too great to cover on foot. A bus map, timetable and tickets are purchased, but hunger is the first requirement to be met, and this is quickly satisfied at the take-away Pizzeria. Wafer thin crust, with meagre, yet delicious topping, folded in half and served in paper, is eaten on the run.

Our first stop, and as it happened the only time we did actually alight from a bus this evening, is at St Peter's Square. I am reminded how vast the cobbled square actually is, and imagine what the expanse must be like when crowded with papal worshippers. Now there are only a few people about and we enjoy the quiet for a few moments, as we lean on a balustrade and watch darkness slowly descend on St Peter's Basilica.

We are not far from the river and figure that from this point, we may as well pick up on the urban trekking option and take a more or less direct route, on foot, to the Colosseum. Walking is a good choice, as it is easier to admire the historic buildings when moving slowly. This is to be a window-shop kind of tour, as at this late hour none of the tourist sites are open.

The Colosseum sits sedately and looks more tranquil than when I saw it last. Back in '75 the ancient amphitheatre was on an island surrounded by roads. Cars and motorbikes zoomed around the island and we had been warned not to walk on the road-edge of the pavement. Thieves passing on motorcycles had been known to take the opportunity to steal handbags hanging from the shoulder nearest to street side. Tonight, with the road redesigned to now only pass-by on three sides, we complete a circumnavigation on foot admiring the hundreds of alcoves bathed in soft light.

In nine hours we have to face our final train ride; just thirty-five kilometres to the Leonardo da Vinci-Fiumicino Airport from where we catch a flight home. In the meantime, the culmination of our evening of site-seeing, is a visit to Trevi Fountain. Nev isn't at all fussed about including the fountain on our schedule, but we are in the vicinity and I would like to celebrate the end of this epic holiday, at the famous landmark. Up until now the evening has been quiet, with few people about. Now we can see that this is because every tourist visiting Rome is standing around Fontana di Trevi. It is hard to believe that so many people are out at this hour; it is eleven o'clock on a week night, and it is not yet peak-tourist season, yet the crowd extends from the water's edge, back deep into the piazza. There is a party atmosphere; noisy excitable chatter and shrieks of laughter, with the occasional shrill whistle penetrating the frivolity, as the guard exerts his official status, whenever someone threatens to put their hand in the water.

Trevi Fountain 1976, Louise is seated on the right-hand corner

Last time Nev and I were in Rome, a visit to the fountain was also on our self-guided tour. The afternoon was quiet then, with only a few people taking any notice of the elaborate statuary and its murky waters. Maybe on that occasion we did toss in a coin, but it is more likely that we did not, as we were just as tight with money, back in our early twenties, as we are now. Also coins were quite rare in Italy at that time. Often we had been given sweets, instead of coins, as change, because there was not the coinage available. It is believed that tossing a coin into the water will eventuate in a future return to Rome, and this tradition is believed to be true by many, as these days around 3000 Euros are collected from the water each day. Maybe it doesn't matter what a person puts into the fountain, the result will still be a return to Rome. I remember on our previous visit that Nev was able to submerge his foot so that he could wash it, and his jandal (New Zealand summer rubber footwear, known as Thongs in Australia) to rid himself of the sticky dog turd he had trodden in. (To this day Nev insists it was human excrement. Back in the 70's a dog turd was white, and this was a brown job). If he attempted an act such as that tonight, he would likely be marched away in handcuffs.

Tonight we don't bother to force our way through the crowds to the fountain waters. Instead of tossing some coins for luck, we spend them on a beer each. A small round table with two chairs has just been vacated, so we are able to sit at a café on the edge of the Piazza. Seated outside on this balmy evening, with a view of the people crowded around the fountain, I focus on enjoying the last moments of this travel experience. Negativities experienced in the past six weeks; hurts, blame, or I told you so, evaporate with the mist that rises from the recirculated tumbling waters.

Sitting companionably together, we form a wish that would have accompanied the coin toss, had we thrown one. It is thirty-one years since we were last here. On that occasion we didn't toss a coin either and yet we have returned. While on that extensive European journey we had spoken of our wishes for a long future together; our hopes for two healthy children, preferably a boy and a girl, and had chosen their names. We have had a fulfilling life to this point, and dwell on our good fortune, with those dreams and so many others, having been realised.

We speak now of returning in another thirty years. Laughing together about the prospect of having our unborn grandchildren bring us back to this city. Maybe then we will be in a tandem wheelchair, two octogenarians, sitting side by side in gentle companionship, with hands gently touching. Our lives, by then, will have been enriched by a wealth of memories, such as those experienced on this tandem ride, and a shared determination to never give up on anything!

About the author

Louise George was born in New Zealand and has called Australia home since 1999. She works full-time as an Information Systems Manager. Her favourite past-times are mountain biking on local trails, and travel that usually includes a few days of mountain biking or tramping. Louise is a wife, and mother of two adult children. This travel memoir is her first narrative of an adventure shared with her husband Nev. Louise lives in Adelaide, South Australia.

Contact: ittakes2totandem@gmail.com

Acknowledgements

Thanks to CTC (http://www.ctc.org.uk) for the comprehensive notes of the YHA route, albeit they were in the opposite LEJOG direction.

To Alex Nutt, of MTB Tandems USA, (http://www.mtbtandems.com) thank you for building our strong sturdy beast named Fandango that safely carried us, the Old Man Mountain racks and loaded Carradice panniers. Also thanks to Schwalbe for the strength of Marathon Plus tyres that clung to the tarmac and kept out the glass and thorns.

Dorothy O'Neil viewed the scanty notes I took during our tandem trip and encouraged me to share my experience. I thank her for teaching me that my writing voice should be spoken with love. While Joyce Graetz didn't read any of my writing, at the age of 82 she wrote 'Amazing Faith', the history of the organisation I work for. Joyce's tenacity inspired me to keep plugging away at the writing task I had set myself. Both women are now living in residential care and I am reminded that life is too short, and we need to make the best of every situation, every day.

For editing advice; my thanks goes to my friends Colleen Jessen and Kay Haarsma, and also to my sister Karrie Brown. Special thanks to Tim Gray, for the 'miracles you worked' with your red pen.
To my son Levi, thank you so much for the cover design.

My love and life-long commitment goes to Nev, who believes in my ability even though I sometimes present self-doubt; and who I know will always be by my side, because he never gives up on anything. Nev your determination has given me a colourful life through the adventures we share.

Printed in Great Britain
by Amazon